THE
Advent
OF
GOD'S
WORD

LISTENING FOR
THE POWER OF TH
DIVINE WHISP

A Daily Retreu
& Devotional

REV. DR. BRENDA K. BUCKWELL, Obl. OSB

CHRISTIAN  JOURNEYS
FROM SKYLIGHT PATHS® PUBLISHING
Woodstock, Vermont

The Advent of God's Word:
Listening for the Power of the Divine Whisper—A Daily Retreat and Devotional
2015 Quality Paperback Edition, First Printing
© 2015 by Brenda K. Buckwell

Library of Congress Cataloging-in-Publication Data
Buckwell, Brenda K., 1957–
The advent of God's word : listening for the power of the divine whisper—a daily retreat and devotional / Rev. Dr. Brenda K. Buckwell, Obl. OSB.
    pages cm
Includes bibliographical references.
ISBN 978-1-59473-576-9 (quality pbk)—ISBN 978-1-59473-615-5 (ebook) 1. Advent. 2. Devotional exercises. 3. Devotional literature. I. Title.
BV40.B763 2015
242'.332—dc23
                                    2015029229

10 9 8 7 6 5 4 3 2 1

Manufactured in the United States of America
Cover design: Jenny Buono
Cover art: © Luba V Nel/Shutterstock
Interior design: Tim Holtz

SkyLight Paths Publishing is creating a place where people of different spiritual traditions come together for challenge and inspiration, a place where we can help each other understand the mystery that lies at the heart of our existence.

SkyLight Paths sees both believers and seekers as a community that increasingly transcends traditional boundaries of religion and denomination—people wanting to learn from each other, *walking together, finding the way.*

SkyLight Paths, "Walking Together, Finding the Way" and colophon are trademarks of LongHill Partners, Inc., registered in the U.S. Patent and Trademark Office.

Walking Together, Finding the Way®
Published by SkyLight Paths Publishing
A Division of LongHill Partners, Inc.
Sunset Farm Offices, Route 4, P.O. Box 237
Woodstock, VT 05091
Tel: (802) 457-4000   Fax: (802) 457-4004
www.skylightpaths.com

Contents

❋ **Week Four**

CELEBRATE! THE POWER OF A WHISPERED LIFE
New Life Springs Forth   113

Acknowledgments

This book would not be possible without the amazing gifts of God's Word, present and creatively shaping my life and prayer. Along with God, many others have assisted in the formation and birthing of this book. First, I thank my family for their faithfulness and sharing the tradition of in-home Advent liturgy with me and allowing me to share our story in part with you. They have encouraged me and supported me through all the years of life and ministry. My friend and mentor Rev. Dr. Dwight Judy has been the voice of God's whispered Word that has provided me confidence and courage to step up to this project as well as many other amazing opportunities for sharing God's prayer and presence through teaching, spiritual direction, and retreat leadership. The heartbeat of stability and faith formation is shared in community prayers with my brothers and sisters in Christ through St. Brigid of Kildare Methodist-Benedictine Monastery, which anoints my written work. I am deeply indebted to my editors, Emily Wichland and Rachel Shields at SkyLight Paths Publishing. Emily was captivated by this book project from my first submission and worked tirelessly sharing her editorial wisdom, support, and care. Without her this book would not have come to publication. Thank you, Emily. And Rachel's attention to detail brought the final creative process to completion. The tremendous vision and collaboration with the design team and editors have made this book a delightful experience of God's power weaving synergy and vision into this published work. I am humbled by this opportunity to share God's prayer and presence with so many. So you, my dear

2

readers, receive my greatest blessing and thanksgiving for your desire to seek and experience God's presence through the words on these pages. May your *adventure* of preparing for Jesus' birth bring you as much joy in the reading as God has granted me in writing.

Introduction

This book is day-by-day experience of the process of Christian spiritual formation. Using the Advent wreath as the focal point for the progression of faith formation and growth, you will be guided to explore the depth and terrain of your heart as we pilgrimage through the four weeks leading up to Jesus' birth on Christmas Day and into the new year. By embarking on this journey, you are choosing to allow the energy and power of God's presence, prayer, and passion to shape your inward nature more closely to the virtues of Jesus. This process is not just for you but always aimed toward increasing faith and relationship with others and toward greater love of God. This book provides an *adventure* of a lifetime—and *for* your lifetime—as we experience a fresh look at Advent resources, incorporate ancient and contemporary spiritual practices, and ponder biblical and historical characters on their faith journey.

The Advent of God's Word has been written just for you! Whether you are deeply immersed in your faith, someone newly drawn to living a life of faith, or looking to become reacquainted with the spiritual rhythms of the Christian calendar and its celebrations, this book is my gift to you. It is also a resource for spiritual directors, directors of spiritual formation, chaplains, retreat and small-group leaders, congregational leaders, and pastors; you will find within these pages support and encouragement for your work as you lead others more intimately into the heart of Christmas.

The weeks leading up to Christmas are often hectic times preparing for the holy celebration of Jesus' birth. This book provides an opportunity for you to pause, take a refreshing breath of the Holy Spirit, and look beyond the surface of the lights and glitter to notice the inward shaping of Jesus' virtues of hope, love, joy, and peace for faithful living. It sets a course for daily retreat and devotional living into the new era for hope and unity in the heart of Christ.

I have spent my entire career as an ordained clergyperson within the United Methodist tradition seeking to integrate Christian spiritual formation into a process of deepening discipleship. I aim to build a solid foundation of prayer and praxis—that is, living out spiritual practices—so that others can experience an expanded sense of God in all aspects of humanity. Over these years, I have engaged in my own holy journey of faith formation and spiritual direction. I have sought mentors in the faith, who taught me ancient prayer practices. Through the ministry of the Fellowship of United Methodist Spiritual Directors and Retreat Leaders: Hearts on Fire, I have led many retreats, workshops, and classes on integrating spiritual formation into everyday life and leadership for the twenty-first-century church. With an ever-deepening quest to know and experience the presence of God, I have found great community and stability of heart as an oblate in Saint Brigid of Kildare Methodist-Benedictine Monastery. My faith quest has been a profound life journey for me that has led to expansion of imagination, creativity, and abiding joy in God. I look forward to walking beside you during this daily retreat as your spiritual director and guide while you embrace this Advent *advent*ure.

A Map of Our Journey Together

Each week of Advent begins with an introduction to the weekly theme. These themes move you from where you currently are in relationship and understanding of God's presence in your life through the difficult choices of life in faith growth into the joy of the Peaceable Kingdom of God dawning in your life on Christmas morning. The introductions have vignettes about Advent and the tradition of family worship and highlight the week's biblical and historical companions for your faith-forming *advent*ure.

Mary, the mother of Jesus, is your constant companion through these weeks. She lives the process of spiritual formation—of God's transformation within the interior of her life to the external shape of her being and relationship with others. The first week you are guided by Mary and Zechariah. With them you will contemplate the interior landscape of your heart. The second week brings Mary, John the Baptist and his mother Elizabeth, and Saint John of the Cross. Once you know the current landscape of your heart from week one, you explore the choices before you in faith formation and how circumstance and choice may lead you into a spiritual struggle known as "the dark night of the soul." As we move deeper and more intentionally into the third week of the Advent formational journey of faith, you are accompanied by Mary and Elizabeth, who find great joy in spiritual friendship and the delight of God's abiding presence. Finally, in the fourth week of Advent, with Christmas birthing near to heart, you are companioned by a cast of characters including the shepherds, Mary, and the wisdom from the ancient desert *ammas* and *abbas*. It is in the fourth week that we experience the fullness of God's passion and love ignited within our hearts as God's Kingdom comes on earth as in heaven.

Each week of Advent also begins with a creative arts experience of prayer. Through the course of my own life and working with many others in spiritual direction, I have found that it is helpful to move beyond the surface presentation of life and seek the interior hidden movements of God. The weekly creative arts prayer experiences are intended to do just this, to move you beyond articulation of what you know of God into greater discernment of the possibilities of Jesus' new birthing in your life. The creative arts prayer practices are icon gazing, *visio divina*, *audio divina*, and meditative movement. For the creative arts prayers you will need Internet access.

Within each week I offer daily devotionals designed with the intent for an extended time of inward formation and prayer. Each includes an inspirational story, biblical references, and a companion story with the daily character. After you prayerfully read the devotional, you have the opportunity to plumb the depths of your heart beyond a surface knowing as you create a pictorial journal of your inward experience of God's prayer and presence.[1] To assist in noticing the interior movement of God, or the quickening of God's activity within your soul, I offer questions to prompt your imagination and expand the dream of God's love becoming an even greater reality within your daily life.

Praying with Mandalas

The French Enlightenment mathematician Blaise Pascal named well the hidden place within each human soul where God resides. He stated that "there is a God-shaped emptiness within each person that only God can fill."[2] The intent of the daily pictorial journal is to assist you in noticing how God yearns within you to fill the God-shaped emptiness so that you can be more deeply formed into the image of Christ.

I believe wholeheartedly that as we pray, God's Spirit within us is praying as well. Mandalas help us set aside our logical, analytic tendencies and better allow the expression of both our spirit and God's Spirit. Creative arts prayer practices in general allow God's Spirit to flow more freely through us. This can lead to beautiful experiences of God's presence and surprising insights and revelations. When I invite you to let the Word of God "write your reflection in the drawing of your mandala" or to "enjoy the creative expression of God," I am referring to this intertwining of spirits. God is whispering the Word, but the Word that is whispered is also full of God's power and presence. "Word" is capitalized throughout this book because it refers to the creative Word of God that spoke in the beginning (Genesis 1), became Incarnate, enfleshed in Jesus (John 1), and is still manifested as Jesus, the creative Word of God, whispering to us during all of life and particularly for this book, during this time of Advent.

The mandala will be used daily to represent the God-shaped emptiness within you and reflect your openness to God's infilling and wisdom from the daily readings and prayer. This sacred circle is an ancient prayer tool. Each major religion has found the mandala useful as a meditative practice that opens space for us to notice the interior movements of God. The mandala depicts oneness with God encircling all of human life and reveals our conscious and unconscious thoughts and feelings, each wrapped by God's prayer and presence through expression of shape and color. There is nothing outside of God's sphere for holy living. Mandalas help us listen with the inner ear of the heart.[3]

Each day you will be invited into your sacred space—a place within your home, workplace, or outside among nature—where you can silently focus upon the interior whispers of God. When you come to your sacred space, you will bring colored pencils or other drawing instruments, a pad of plain drawing paper for the creation of your pictorial journal, and a lined notebook for journaling. These tools will assist you with your beyond-the-word articulation of God's interior shaping of your Advent *advent*ure. Be encouraged. God will provide color, imagination, and a wordless whisper of Jesus' creative Word when you turn your intention to deeper listening.

To create a mandala, first draw a circle. The empty circle is your canvas for prayer and a symbol of your desire to be open to the whispers of God's power and presence this Advent season. Then, using colored pencils, crayons, or other drawing instruments, create an abstract expression or realistic, or concrete, image within the circle. These marks on the page express unconscious feelings, thoughts, nudges, and whispers of God. There are no correct techniques for drawing. Simply express what your heart is feeling through color and doodles within the circle to give birth to your mandala. You need no artistic ability, only the desire to listen beyond the printed word and to express your wordless experience of God's presence. This prayer practice is one way the Spirit intercedes for us with sighs too deep for words (Romans 8:26). May God's Word be whispered and welcomed into your heart during this holy time of retreat to fill the God-shaped emptiness within your hungering soul.

To gain the greatest insight from the mandala, it is often helpful to gaze at the completed drawing in the same way we would gaze upon an icon. This gazing upon our spirit's creation assists us in assimilating what God is speaking through the mandala. As you reflect and pray upon your completed mandala, you may want to record any thoughts or words that come to mind in your written journal. Journaling is your opportunity to ask God for further wisdom and insight into what you have drawn on the mandala. You may ask questions of God, wondering what a certain color expresses or what the shapes depict for you as God anoints your prayer art and God's Spirit intercedes for you with sighs and wordless expression. As you reflect upon your completed mandala, you might write one word inside the mandala itself or whole phrases or sentences around your mandala's edge. In the example below, my mandala shows ribbons flying from the cross and dancing musical notes. The ribbons represent freedom. The musical notes suggest a new song being sung within my life.

You may experience anxiety with the mention of a pictorial journal. Not many of us are professional artists. I assure you, neither am I! Yet I find expressing my soul through color and marks on a page gives great insight into God's wordless whispers to my heart. No professional or even semi-professional artistic skill is needed for this project. Simply a desire to experience God's prayer and presence beyond the articulated word qualifies you as an artist of the spirit. We are spiritual beings that long for expression. Expression of the spiritual life is more than just head knowledge. The heart expands in God's love as expression is gifted to the spirit through these wordless images within your pictorial journal.

Carrying the Experience into the New Year

Following the four weeks of Advent and the Christmas Day celebratory devotionals, a three-part epilogue sends you into the new year with an intentional rhythm of daily, weekly, and annual prayer. First you will discover your covenant renewal prayer to anchor your heart in prayer for the new year. Next you will search your heart to set up your "Rule of Life" for a covenant of commitment to prayer and spiritual practices. With the solid foundation of a personal covenant renewal prayer and your Rule of Life, you will discover the foundational scripture that guides your daily life—your biblical DNA. Through these three simple exercises you lay a foundation for daily devotion into the new year, and through this rhythm of prayer you will find stability, great joy, and blessing in God's ever-present power in your life.

The concluding portion of the book is the leader's guide. This guide provides instruction for using *The Advent of God's Word* in face-to-face and online small-group opportunities. An outline of weekly retreat gatherings encourages group times of silence for participants to experience the weekly creative arts prayer, discussion options for the weekly theme, and practical ideas for sharing the faith journey of each participant. I have suggested two distinct formats. One option is to have a three-hour retreat to experience each of the practices of covenant renewal prayer, creating a Rule of Life, and biblical DNA. The other suggested option provides for three one-hour retreats to experience these three disciplines one at a time. Either way, the small group will be sent off into the new year with a steadfast rhythm of God's prayer and contemplative practices.

Enhanced Online Prayer Experience

Throughout the book are instructions for exploring web-based resources. These resources may be found by searching for the topic given in the daily devotions or by using the provided links that may be entered directly into your browser. You may use the suggested resources or others you choose. For example, when the creative arts prayer experience calls for viewing a video, you may select a video you have or can access through your television or online. I provide instructions in the daily devotions for viewing and praying with the enhanced online options for retreating.

Entering into Sacred Space

The time has come, dear companions, to begin your Advent *advent*ure! As you will learn through the pages of this book, Advent has always been a very special season for me. I pray that you may experience the presence of God's gentle nudges guiding you and whispering to your heart as the Divine power and presence of God illumines these weeks of holy birthing within your heart. I look forward to walking beside you as you discover the gift of Jesus' new birthing in your life this year.

To begin, please consider your sacred space for retreat as you read the daily devotionals and create your pictorial journal. A quiet and safe space for contemplative prayer assists in settling the spirit into devotional reading and reflection. If you have not already designated a space for prayer in either your home or workplace, take time before beginning the practices in this book to choose an area. Perhaps this will be near your favorite comfortable chair. You may wish to create a simple altar to help you focus in your prayer and contemplation. Here are a few suggestions.

- Begin your search for a sacred space by asking God for guidance.
- Once you find a specific room or corner of a room, choose a chair. Some people prefer a straight-backed chair that calls the body to attention before God rather than a cushy, comfortable chair. Either is fine as long as your spirit can breathe in that space.
- Secure a small table for your altar, which may be as simple or elaborate as you like. Consider these ideas:
  - Drape the table with scarves, a tablecloth, or other fabric.
  - Place on the table a Bible and a personal item that represents a special moment on your spiritual journey, such as a rock, feather, or live plant.
  - Keep a candle and matches on the table, so as you begin your time of deep daily listening for God's whispers, you can light the candle, praying for God's light and presence to illumine your time of prayer.
- Once you have created your sacred space, offer a prayer of thanksgiving and anointing of this space.

May God's holy blessing be poured out upon you as you pray and listen for God's whispers through this Advent retreat and daily devotional book. Sit back, enjoy, and receive God's anointing as Jesus' new birth becomes reality in your life. As we begin this *adven*ture, let us draw our hearts together in prayer:

Holy One, Holy Three, encircle us across the miles and mold us into companions for this journey toward your divine birthing. Cause all resistance within us to fade away. Expand our desire for you. Ignite the flame of passion within as we listen for your whispers wooing and forming us ever more nearly into your image. May we become your vessels, sharing the fruits of this retreat and daily devotional prayer with all whom we encounter in our everyday living. We love you. We long for you. With expectant hearts and yearning souls, we watch and wait to experience your surprising and mysterious Word and energy transforming our lives as we journey toward the manger in anticipation of Jesus' birth. Amen.

Blessing on the Way,
Brenda

THE TERRAIN FOR WHISPERS

Discerning the Landscape of the Heart

*From fertile valley to barren cliffs Jesus' Word is spoken
into new possibility and the whispering cry is heard:
"Awake, my soul, that I may soar upon joy of the morning."*

Since earliest memory, Advent has been a special and holy season for me. Every year my parents gathered my siblings and me around the Advent wreath, which sat center stage in the living room on the coffee table. It was a symbol of the expectation and anticipation of the new birth of Jesus. It signified getting ready for Christmas! By the time I was old enough to read, I orchestrated our weekly Advent home wreath-lighting worship celebrations. Boldly I assigned parts. One would read scripture, another would read the weekly poem or inspirational story, and still another lit the appropriate candle or candles coinciding with the week of Advent we were celebrating. My heart was captivated by the flickering flame of Divine love, the holy scripture, and the way God's awesome presence knit our family together during those special moments. Once the last prayer was said and the celebration came to a close, laughter rang out as we burst into rousing choruses of every Christmas song we knew! Off-key as we were, the celebration held great beauty and mystery of God's power and presence within my heart.

Traditionally a Lutheran practice, lighting the Advent wreath during the four weeks of preparation leading up to the birth of Jesus on Christmas has found a place of honor in most Western Christian churches. The Advent wreath is traditionally created by placing pine boughs in a circle, with four candles arising from the evergreens. The candles are symmetrically placed around the circle, creating a circumference of light and beauty. Each Sunday a candle is lit until the four candles around the circle fully illumine the boughs. I remember as a young child the colors of these four candles being red, but over time tradition has claimed these candles to be three purple and one pink. In the center of the wreath is a white candle, which is the Christ candle. The Christ candle is the final candle of the wreath and is lit on Christmas Eve or Christmas Day to celebrate the birth of Jesus.

On the first Sunday of Advent a purple candle is lit. Sometimes described as the "prophecy candle," this candle is traditionally known to represent hope and expectation. For me, lighting this first candle is a symbol of the intentional desire to journey toward the birth of Jesus with an ever-opening heart. This inward journey of the heart begins right where you are. Taking time to assess the landscape of the heart and notice the interior shifts of feelings, thoughts, attitudes, hopes, and dreams of the heart's transformational journey over the next four weeks is the reflective-retreat pause of the Advent season.

Your Companions This Week

As you begin your inward journey of the heart this week, you are accompanied by two biblical figures who exemplify for us differing landscapes of heart—Mary, Jesus' mother, and Zechariah, husband to Mary's cousin Elizabeth. It is this week that we often read the Gospel passage of Luke 1:26–38, in which Mary hears the power of the Divine whisper as she consents to become pregnant by God's very presence. Can you imagine what it was like for Mary, thirteen or fourteen years of age, on the edge of womanhood, as the energy and power of God's new life began growing within her? Just hearing from the angel Gabriel and being hailed as one anointed by God, favored and chosen to bear God's son, could have so surprised Mary that she could have become paralyzed with fear of what God was about to do within her life. She could have tried to deny miraculous logic with human logic or sought to hide from God. She could have pretended she only imagined the conversation with the Divine. And yet when God came to her and offered her the possibility of bearing Jesus, Mary said "Yes!" Mary stepped into the mystery of God's activity within her life. Mary's inward journey of formation by the God-shaping energy present in her life shifted as her dreams of "someday" becoming a mother became "now." Her dreams for a wedding and family feasting turned to "now?" as she may have wondered how to tell her Divine encounter story and to whom she could turn with such precious news. Her self-image began to shift on the inside as her pregnancy steadily changed her outside physical shape. In the here and now of the present moment, the annunciation of Jesus' birth changed the landscape of Mary's heart.

A companion story of annunciation is told in Luke 1:5–25. Mary's cousin Elizabeth was married to a devout priest named Zechariah. When the Word of God was whispered in the fullness of power and possibility to Zechariah that his seemingly barren wife would become pregnant and bear a son to be named John, Zechariah had a different reaction than Mary when the Word of God was whispered to him in the temple. Zechariah asked the angel for proof: "How will I know that this is so? For I am an old man, and my wife is getting on in years" (Luke 1:18). Mary, on the other hand, stepped into the wonder of mystery at how such a miracle could happen to her. "How can this be," Mary asked the angel, "since I am a virgin?" (Luke 1:34). And God responded differently to the two human hearts. Zechariah was struck into silence until the birth of his son, John the Baptist. And Mary was gifted with the proof that God can and does create miraculous life by being told that her cousin Elizabeth was pregnant.

Wonders arise for me: What was the interior longing of Zechariah's heart? How did he hold fast in faith through years of disappointment and barrenness for his wife? Had the numerous years of Elizabeth's barrenness hardened his heart's imagination to the possibilities of God's miraculous intervention in human life? What inward landscape of heart *did* Zechariah have as the power of the Divine whisper created new life within his family? However these wonders are answered, one thing I am sure of—God came to Zechariah exactly in the current emotions, feelings, and circumstances of his daily living.

Your Inward Journey

Just as with Mary and Zechariah, your own inward journey of the heart begins this week, right where you are. Whatever longings, burdens, stressors, or joys fill daily living, or whatever attitudes and thoughts affect your behavior, this is the exact right moment and place for Jesus to meet you in your personal life. Jesus comes to each of us in our yearning for something more and in our anticipation of the possibilities that arise as the Advent *advent*ure begins. The most mystifying work of God begins as God opens space within the heart for Divine love to gently shape the interior landscape of your heart.

This week, as you begin your spiritual journey, pause for an intentional time away from the rush of Christmas hustle and bustle and wonder about the current landscape of your heart. Consider the interior thoughts that run through your mind. Contemplate the effect of emotions as they shape the terrain of your heart. By consciously noticing your present spiritual landscape, you are preparing your heart to allow the Divine power, energy, love, and presence of Jesus to gently shape your inward nature to become more Christ-like. It is in the present moment, the here and now of life, that the formation of Jesus' new birthing begins. As you become aware of the condition of your heart, the resistances, hopes, joys, fears, and dreams—the gifts of God's new possibilities—are sown in the depths of your heart. It is then that Jesus' love blossoms into even greater potential. Together we venture into the *advent*ure of Advent. May God's surprises of new birthing be announced into your interior heart just where you are this week.

THE FIRST SUNDAY OF ADVENT:
A CREATIVE ARTS PRAYER PRACTICE

Icon Gazing: Praying with the Soft Eyes of God

Incarnation, the Word of God becoming flesh, captivated my heart as I gazed at the illumination hanging in the lobby of Saint John's Abbey in Collegeville, Minnesota.[1] My soul leapt with yearning as the insistent call to become even more Christ-like arose within my heart. This prayer filled my heart from the depths of the literal presence of God, which shined forth from the handcrafted picture called an illumination. It was calling me to contemplate how to live more intentionally into a love like Jesus' love as I relate to others within the world. Instantly I realized this as the process of Christian spiritual formation birthing new potential within me, as I gazed at this brilliance of God's drawn Word. I recognized God's slight shifting of the landscape of my heart radiating the depth of Jesus' compassion and love in service to the world. It is this indwelling of Incarnation that anchors the love song and powerful whispers of God's Word as we enter into Advent. God's Word does indeed seek to transform the landscape of our heart.

My experience at Saint John's Abbey is an example of icon gazing, a specific creative prayer practice of seeing God's Word beyond the surface. Viewing art with prayerful anticipation and expectation of noticing God's powerful presence is for me "praying with the soft eyes of God," an expression I learned in spiritual direction training. Gazing or praying with the soft eyes of God draws the heart and the center of my being to see artwork, a person, or circumstance from God's loving perspective. It asks me to let go of my own perspective and expectations—my desired outcomes. It requires me to hold objects or relationships lightly, to not choke creativity or other opinions and options out of possibility. This deep gaze of love causes me to pause and wonder while I look upon a person, place, or thing: "How does Jesus view and live within this beloved person, object, or piece of art in front of me?" "How has Jesus' loving presence been prayed into this piece of art by the iconographer?" "Is there an increased experience and understanding of God that I can glean from this encounter?" "Is there more to this situation or piece of art than I saw at first glance?" Gazing with the soft eyes of God provides the gentle expansion of imagination and possibilities.

Icons exist to help connect a person or people to God. From the inception of its creation, the icon is bathed in prayer. The iconographer or illuminator (the one writing the Word of God) has prayed with each stroke of the pen, asking God to anoint the icon with God's living and creative power so that God's whispered Word may speak directly to all future viewers of the image. Your connection occurs as you take extended time to view the illumination of God's Word. Your prayerful heart is literally drawn into the picture through this living Word of God. This is similar to the power and presence of God's living Word, which dwells in scripture and captivates your mind and heart as you read and pray the words of scripture. Every icon is written with a focal point that catches the viewer's spirit and lures the viewer's soul into deepened knowing and understanding of God's presence. Both icons and mandalas are "written," not "drawn," because they are a visible entryway to experiencing the living Word of God.

The Challenges of Icon Gazing

A difficulty that often rears its power, particularly if you are new to icon gazing, is indifference. If you are indifferent to the image of God in the piece of art that you are looking at, you will most likely not experience the presence of God in the icon. To be indifferent is to look at people, objects, art, and situations of life only from our own human agenda and perspective without the thought or mental wonder of what God may be whispering through the circumstance, picture, or person. Indifference to the image of God arises when you rush through icon gazing without expectation of the Divine presence. Giving only a quick glance to an icon is one-dimensional viewing, seeing only the shapes and colors that are on the surface of the image. When you take extended time to sit in silence with an internal posture of expectation and prayer, awaiting God's presence to emerge from the artistic icon, then you will not be disappointed.

The most important role of icons in Christian history is to proclaim the physical reality of Jesus Christ. When Jesus was crucified, buried, and rose from the dead, the opportunity for the unleashing of his Spirit was breathed into humanity. It is the power and presence of the Holy Spirit of Jesus that is manifest through gazing upon sacred art with this prayer practice of icon gazing.

In the commotion of Christmas preparations it is easy to be over-whelmed with distractions. Icons can quiet the deafening white noise of society and the harried scurry of this season, silencing the soul into a receptive posture ready to notice the activity of God. The intentional focus and prayer you have while wondering what word God will speak through the icon actually opens the way for your spirit to be drawn into the picture through a felt sense of God's essence. This mysterious, hidden, unspoken Word of God wooing the soul through icon gazing *is* seeking beyond the surface of words and listening with the inner ear of the heart to the power of the Divine whisper.

The intent of today's creative arts experience is for you simply to notice the prayer that wells up within as you gaze lovingly, with the hope and anticipation of experiencing God's presence through icon gazing.

Practicing Icon Gazing

Plan at least thirty minutes for this prayer practice.

On this first Sunday of Advent, you may choose to sit attentively looking at any picture that captures your heart's attention. You may choose to gaze at a print or painting that has previously caught your attention and now may be hanging on the wall of your home. For an enhanced online option of icon gazing, you may desire to pray with the picture that caught my heart from the Saint John's Bible. You can find this image by searching online for "Saint John's Bible Word became flesh illumination" or by entering the following link into your browser: https://goo.gl/TdkGDX. If you do not have Internet access, your local library likely has works of art for further icon-gazing prayers.

As you come into your sacred space, offer a prayer anointing this space. Bring to your consciousness the possibility and expectation that in this space you will hear God's whispers to your heart through gazing with the soft eyes of God. You may use this prayer or one of your own for anointing your sacred space:

> Holy Jesus, pour out your Spirit upon this space. For the next four weeks, as I sit in this place, may I gain a felt sense of your presence encircling my thoughts, prayers, drawing, and writing so that I may notice you even more deeply within these times of prayer. Thank you, Jesus, for this holy and sacred space, as I seek to become more mindful of you throughout this season, as your advent dawns in my life. Amen.

To begin, sit comfortably, and focus your eyes and heart upon the icon. Take a few deep, cleansing breaths as you sit quietly, preparing to gaze at the icon. Breathe in slowly, drawing the Spirit of God into your awareness. Let God's Spirit fill your lungs with the creative possibility of God's vision. Slowly exhale all resistance and busyness from your day, leaving space for God to fill your heart and imagination. Release any indifference or resistance within you, allowing your heart to experience the allure of God's love drawing you into the picture. Remember Blaise Pascal's image from this book's introduction that all humans are created with a God-shaped emptiness within us that only God can fill, so releasing resistances and busyness assists in making the heart ready to receive God.

As you wait in this space, expanding the emptiness and openness within you before God, invite God to speak to you through your chosen icon. Trust that God's Word is creatively present in order to speak directly to your heart.

To assist in this gazing prayer, I have provided a few thoughtful questions to stir the imagination and expand awareness of God's presence.

- ⊕ How does God invite you into this picture?
- ⊕ What is it about this icon that draws your heart's attention?
- ⊕ How do you imagine what you are most drawn to in this picture could be God's voice whispering a wooing love song to your heart?
- ⊕ What is God saying to you through this icon?
- ⊕ What could this picture be telling you about the current terrain of your heart?
- ⊕ How does hope spring from the icon into your prayer?

Your Mandala: Listening Beyond Words for the Power of a Divine Whisper

The creation of your mandala is the daily retreat throughout this devotional book. It takes intentional time, focus, and prayer to allow God to silence all distractions of heart and create your mandala. From your icon-gazing prayer exercise, consider the landscape of your heart. What feelings, thoughts, and wordless wonders could your spirit be holding that you are not yet aware of? No need to try to articulate these wordless insights of God's powerful whisper; simply creating marks and colors on the page can give them expression. I invite you to draw your empty mandala circle as a symbol of the God-shaped emptiness within your soul. This empty space within the heart is where you experience Jesus' new Christmas birthing. As you fill the circle with color, your first step of discernment in giving expression to the terrain of your heart, you begin your Advent journey. You will focus on the terrain of your heart all this first week. By the end of this Advent retreat you will have created a pictorial journal providing God's wordless whisper and power to you at this time in your life as you celebrate Jesus' birth at Christmas.

Gather your tools of illumination: journal, pen, sketch pad, and colored pencils. Come into God's presence and settle yourself into your sacred space. After your time of gazing upon the icon, take your sketch pad and prayerfully draw your sacred circle for the creation of your mandala for today. As you gaze at the beauty of the empty space, ponder God's possibilities.

- As you begin the creation of your mandala, you may choose to consider:
  - What color represents the feeling of your spirit after gazing upon the icon?
  - How has this icon inspired your spirit?
  - How did you notice the shimmering of God's illumination?
  - What sensations, thoughts, energies, emotions arise within you as you notice the dawning of God's presence and invitation to you through this icon?
  - What colors best express these energies and emotions?
- As you let the Word of God write your reflections through the drawing of your mandala, consider abstract expression, concrete images, or a mixture of both in the creation of your mandala.

Pause here to create your mandala, expressing the felt sense of God's prayer and presence that you experienced during your gazing upon the icon of your choosing.

When you have completed your prayerful gazing upon the creative arts icon and the creation of your mandala, offer a silent prayer of thanksgiving to God for new insights and wonders that have crossed your mind during this prayer and the experience of creating your first mandala.

The Shimmering Word

John 1:1–5, 14

> In the beginning was the Word ...
>
> John:1–1

... that creative Word of God, which spoke the world into existence.

I was in a coaching conversation the week I wrote this devotional. I told my story. The coach listened. The conversation had its time of give and take, reflection and silence, excitement and hesitant pause while thoughts were gathered. After a time of ebb and flow in conversation, the coach spoke the creative Word of God. The question she asked caused my heart to leap. New imagination and insight ignited within me. The power of God's creative force slowly began to be unleashed and a fresh perspective came into existence, creating a new pathway for the next steps of my journey.

> In the beginning was the Word, and the Word was with God, and the Word was God. He was in the beginning with God. All things came into being through him, and without him not one thing came into being. What has come into being in him was life, and the life was the light of all people. The light shines in the darkness, and the darkness did not overcome it.
>
> John 1:1–5

That day, as the coach and I spoke, the dawning of God's creative Word called forth expanded imagination, birthing possibility within the veiled places of my mind. The shimmering light of God's hope began to dance in my heart. The steps were simple and yet profound. It began with the acknowledgment that someone understood my inward thoughts. What great joy of spirit leapt to the beat of my heart! The joy of knowing what is most profound, where God has secretly knit me together, is not mine alone, but is common to humanity. The dance continued. Where my imagination had previously been restricted, diminished by self-imposed barriers, I found my heart was no longer limited in what could be possible. The dawning of God's light illumined the darkness of the constraints of my former thinking. The advent of new possibilities expanded within me. Freedom danced, hope was born, and the journey to new perspective began.

> And the Word became flesh and lived among us, and we have seen
> his glory, the glory as of a father's only son, full of grace and truth.
> John 1:14

As we enter the Advent season, the hope of God's possibilities seeps into our being. The Advent journey is one of looking at both resistances and places of un-freedom in our lives. We *also* look for the dawning glimmers of God's light, calling forth our attention as the Spirit sweeps over us, illumining the way through even the thickets, brambles, and briars of our lives.

Ꮓ Your Mandala: Listening Beyond Words for the Power of a Divine Whisper

Gather your tools of illumination: journal, pen, sketch pad, and colored pencils. Come into God's presence and settle yourself into your sacred space. Upon your sketch pad prayerfully draw your sacred circle for the creation of your mandala for today. As you gaze at the beauty of the empty space, ponder God's possibilities.

- ⊕ Pause. Center yourself by breathing deeply of God's infilling Spirit, letting go of all resistances and negativity within your heart.
- ⊕ Reread John 1:1–5, 14.
- ⊕ Let the colors of your spirit flow into the mandala as you begin to draw, considering:
    - ✤ When have you encountered the darkness trying to snuff out the light, and yet the light was not overtaken by darkness?
    - ✤ How did you notice the shimmering of God's illumination?

⚜ What sensations, thoughts, energies, emotions arise within you as you notice the dawning of God's light?

⊕ As you let the Word of God write your reflections in the drawing of your mandala, ponder the hope of Advent's dawning.

  ⚜ Prayerfully choose what colors you are drawn to.

  ⚜ Consider abstract expression, concrete images, or a mixture of both in the creation of your mandala.

  ⚜ How does the choice of colors reflect your choices on the spiritual path at this stage of your Advent *adventure*?

I encourage you to strive to create a mandala for each daily reflection. This pictorial journey of reflection beyond words will awaken new possibility through God's wooing whispers as you listen for the advent of God's power and invitation to you this holy season.

Sit back and receive the anointing as the dawning of God's new birth becomes reality in your life. Enjoy the creative expression of God. If creating a mandala for today fails to inspire your heart, consider writing a journal entry, poem, or prayer to express God's illumination of your new pathway and possibilities

Upon completion of your mandala, while gazing with the soft eyes of God upon your mandala, offer a silent prayer of gratitude for the Word whispered from God.

Topography and Terrain

Luke 1:26–31, 34–38
Luke 1:5–13, 18–20

Many folks think the landscape of flat, dull Ohio, landlocked in the middle of the country, is *boring*, especially if you are making a four-hour drive east or west across the state. There is little change in the scenery. But the history of Ohio's topography is one that causes me to marvel at the mystery and forces of nature. Years ago, as the Ice Age imprinted the world, glaciers slowly crept down from the north and flattened the entire state. Ahead of the creeping glaciers, the rocks, soil, plants—everything in the glaciers' path—were bulldozed. Deposits of earth mounds were created at the glaciers' farthest reaching point. As the earth slowly warmed, the melting glaciers receded toward the frigid poles of the earth. Ohio emerged as a land filled with black swamps. The winds blew. The sun shone. And the seasons changed through the years as rich and fertile land emerged.

Folks don't flock to Ohio to view picturesque rock formations or a sweeping expanse of the ocean. However, as you hike through the woods, looking with expectation and wonder, you experience the beauty of God's creation. From the vistas of overpasses to the bustle of the metropolitan areas, the terrain of life is filled with awe and wonder. The topography of Ohio is quilted with natural parks and fields throughout the countryside; its skylines are dotted with buildings reaching up to the sky and flecked by homes in urban metropolises.

Topography isn't just a surface-level phenomenon. It is below the surface that power and energy gather, shaking the earth's surface as the earthquake breaks open the ground and forms cracks and deep crevasses. Just below the surface, the nutrients within the soil seep into the roots of ecological systems, nourishing the seeds of the earth. Topography is an interesting field of study, especially when you consider how the interior or subsurface movements shape the exterior form and landscape.

Every person has his or her own topography, shaped at the sub-surface level—the topography of the heart. It begins with the layers of life under the surface, as motivations, feelings, and attitudes are formed in our inward being. This hidden shaping of character affects outward expression. The interior attitude generates the power and energy that can explode into the outward life as judgment, anger, and resentments or as laughter, love, and joy. This is how we are formed from the inside out by the power and presence of God's shaping love. This is what happens throughout our lives as we are formed by God into our most authentic Christ-like person. This process is Christian spiritual formation. It is here in the terrain of the heart that God nourishes the seeds of our earthly life.

Consider the terrain of your heart. What does the landscape look like in the hidden depths (or heights) of your heart? Are there resentments staining the terrain of your heart or sorrows restricting the depths of your faith? Do joy and hope illumine every corner of your heart? As you step further into this first week of Advent, consider the topography of your inward being.

How prepared are you to receive the good news of Jesus' birth? What *is* the terrain of your heart? With these questions, I am reminded of the parable of the sower (Matthew 13:1–9). The sower spread seed upon the land. Some of the land was receptive; in other places, the seeds got trampled or mixed in with weeds; still other seeds met with the hard, resistant earth or with the earth's good soil. Advent becomes a season of sowing the seeds of God's birthing into humanity. Today, consider exactly where you are. Is the soil of your heart's terrain ready to receive the seeds that are God's love? Are you ready to enter into this holy season of expectation? God's advent dawns into life exactly where we are.

Ponder the following passages from scripture and imagine what the topography and the terrain of Mary's and Zechariah's hearts may have been as the Word of God whispered to their hearts.

Mary

In the sixth month the angel Gabriel was sent by God to a town in Galilee called Nazareth, to a virgin engaged to a man whose name was Joseph, of the house of David. The virgin's name was Mary. And he came to her and said, "Greetings, favored one! The Lord is with you."

But she was much perplexed by his words and pondered what sort of greeting this might be. The angel said to her, "Do not be afraid, Mary, for you have found favor with God. And now, you will conceive in your womb and bear a son, and you will name him Jesus...."

Mary said to the angel, "How can this be, since I am a virgin?" The angel said to her, "The Holy Spirit will come upon you, and the power of the Most High will overshadow you; therefore the child to be born will be holy; he will be called Son of God. And now, your relative Elizabeth in her old age has also conceived a son; and this is the sixth month for her who was said to be barren. For nothing will be impossible with God." Then Mary said, "Here am I, the servant of the Lord; let it be with me according to your word." Then the angel departed from her.

Luke 1:26–31, 34–38

Zechariah

In the days of King Herod of Judea, there was a priest named Zechariah, who belonged to the priestly order of Abijah. His wife was a descendant of Aaron, and her name was Elizabeth. Both of them were righteous before God, living blamelessly according to all the commandments and regulations of the Lord. But they had no children, because Elizabeth was barren, and both were getting on in years.

Once when he was serving as priest before God and his section was on duty, he was chosen by lot, according to the custom of the priesthood, to enter the sanctuary of the Lord and offer incense. Now at the time of the incense-offering, the whole assembly of the people was praying outside. Then there appeared to him an angel of the Lord, standing at the right side of the altar of incense. When Zechariah saw him, he was terrified; and fear overwhelmed him. But the angel said to him, "Do not be afraid, Zechariah, for your prayer has been heard. Your wife Elizabeth will bear you a son, and you will name him John...." Zechariah said to the angel, "How will I know that this is so? For I am an old man, and my wife is getting on in years." The angel replied, "I am Gabriel. I stand in the presence of God, and I have been sent to speak to you and to bring you this good news. But now, because you did not believe my words, which will be fulfilled in their time, you will become mute, unable to speak, until the day these things occur."

Luke 1:5–13, 18–20

Today, spend some meditative time contemplating Mary's and Zechariah's encounters with God's powerful, creative, and transforming Word, whispering new reality into their lives. Imagine beyond the text what the terrain and topography of Mary's and Zechariah's hearts may have been. To begin this imaginative prayer experience, invite God into your reading of the texts. Ask God to expand your imagination and to grant you a new perspective in hearing these very familiar words of scripture.

For me, I can imagine both Mary's and Zechariah's hearts as places of fertile ground for the living seed of God to be sowed. I imagine this rich terrain of fertile ground as a place of waiting and trusting God. Yet I wonder if there is a difference in posture of faith between Mary and Zechariah. Could Zechariah unknowingly be clinging to disappointments, resentments, or sorrows from his great desire for a child and the many years of barrenness that he and his wife, Elizabeth, experienced? I imagine creating a mandala for Zechariah in which most of the circle is filled with the illumination of God's presence, yet the darkness of disappointment or resentment lurks around the edges.

Mary's mandala for my imagination pulses with radiance, even though there is the same response—"Do not be afraid"—from the angel. My imagination finds only joy, hope, the dance of possibility and trust in God's guidance beyond whatever difficulties may arise. In this mandala, I imagine the illumination of God's presence casts out all darkness and doubt.

❧ Your Mandala: Listening Beyond Words for the Power of a Divine Whisper

Gather your tools of illumination: journal, pen, sketch pad, and colored pencils. Come into God's presence and settle yourself into your sacred space. Upon your sketch pad prayerfully draw your sacred circle for the creation of your mandala for today. As you gaze at the beauty of the empty space, ponder God's possibilities.

- ⊕ Pause. Center yourself by breathing deeply of God's infilling Spirit, letting go of all resistances and negativity within your heart.
- ⊕ Consider: Topography is not just a surface-level phenomenon of your life experienced through the outward expression of actions, words, and interpersonal relationships. Topography is formed by the layers of life under the surface—motivations, feelings, attitudes—and how these inward expressions are lived out in our encounters with others.
- ⊕ Let the colors of your spirit flow into the mandala as you begin to draw, considering:
  - ✤ How prepared are you to receive the good news of Jesus' birth?
  - ✤ What does the terrain of your heart look like?
  - ✤ What colors best capture the inward expressions of your heart's terrain?
- ⊕ As you let the Word of God write your reflections in the drawing of your mandala, ponder the hope of Advent's dawning.
  - ✤ Prayerfully choose what colors you are drawn to.
  - ✤ Consider abstract expression, concrete images, or a mixture of both in the creation of your mandala.
  - ✤ How does the choice of colors reflect your choices on the spiritual path at this stage of your Advent *advent*ure?

I encourage you to strive to create a mandala for each daily reflection. This pictorial journey of reflection beyond words will awaken new possibility through God's wooing whispers as you listen for the advent of God's call this holy season.

Sit back and receive the anointing as the dawning of God's new birth becomes reality in your life. Enjoy the creative expression of God. If creating a mandala for today fails to inspire your heart, consider writing a journal entry, poem, or prayer to express the interior terrain of your heart.

Upon completion of your mandala, offer a silent prayer of gratitude for this time of conversation with God and for the hope that is possible as God continues you on this *advent*ure.

Prepare the Way of the Lord

Isaiah 40:3–5

A voice cries out:
"In the wilderness prepare the way of the Lord,
make straight in the desert a highway for our God.
Every valley shall be lifted up,
and every mountain and hill be made low;
the uneven ground shall become level,
and the rough places a plain.
Then the glory of the Lord shall be revealed,
and all people shall see it together,
for the mouth of the Lord has spoken."
　　Isaiah 40:3–5

These words from the prophet Isaiah came alive for me on a bright sunny day in August as the glory of the Lord was revealed. Before I go any further, there is one thing I must confess: I am afraid of heights. I have been told that when I was two years old, I climbed on top of a rock in the backyard (maybe knee high—after all, how high can a toddler climb?). I looked around and began to scream. I was too high up. I couldn't get down. Surely in my two-year-old mind the world was going to come to an end, and I would come crashing down.

　　I have come to look upon my irrational fear of heights with tenderness and kindness. It is a great humbling act to need to jump onto an escalator in the midst of a busy airport and know that when I do, my knees may get weak as in my mind's eye my body simply is projected over the side of the handrail. It is humbling indeed to ask a stranger if she could please ride up immediately behind me—nearly touching my back on the trip to the top—giving me a sense of stability. Over the years, I have worked on overcoming this slightly disabling irrational fear. And a few years ago I thought, "Wow, I am getting much better. I don't think I am afraid of heights anymore!"

On that bright sunny day in August, my courageous proclamation of fearlessness crossed my mind as I was on pilgrimage driving across the mountains of West Virginia, Pennsylvania, Maryland, and on to the East Coast. In fact, I was feeling so confident with my newfound freedom of not being afraid of heights that as I crossed one very long bridge, I wondered what was beneath me and I looked over! I never did figure out what I was driving over. What caught my line of sight in the distance caused my heart to jump into my throat. I saw that this enormously huge concrete bridge was suspended by one lone support beam at the height of the bridge. Immediately I realized I would have to drive back over that bridge on my way home. My fear of heights loomed larger than life and held me captive. Even so, with my fears, through prayer and God's grace I reached my destination without incident.

But that bridge! That suspended white concrete bridge haunted me. Each night I awoke with panic attacks, seeing the bridge. During my wakeful hours the thought plagued me: what if I had a panic attack driving on the bridge and wrecked the car, killing someone? I sought directions to find another route home, but to no avail. Alas, I knew I must drive across the bridge. The night before my return trip home, I attended a Taizé prayer and healing worship celebration. The gentleman who prayed with me prayed the bridge might be shielded from my sight. That night I slept well for first time since crossing the bridge.

As I drove home, viewing the mountain range, dread filled my being. I knew as I approached the mountain the bridge would quickly be before me. I began the incline up, and in that instant Isaiah's words sprang to life. The sensation of going up the mountain stopped. The scenery out the window changed. The mountains transformed into cornfields. The valleys were raised up, the mountains pulled down. For the hour drive across that mountain range I watched, anticipated, and prayed, expecting to experience that white concrete bridge at any moment. Lo and behold, the miles clicked down and the cornfields remained my companions through the entire journey. At the end of the hour on that stretch of highway, as I descended the mountaintop I felt the downward slope of the mountain. The beauty of the mountains shone in my rearview mirror, and I was humbled by the glory of God's highway. I know that I crossed that bridge—there was no other way home. But just as the pray-er stated the night before, the bridge was shielded from my sight.

> A voice cries out:
> "In the wilderness prepare the way of the Lord,
> make straight in the desert a highway for our God.
> Every valley shall be lifted up,
> and every mountain and hill be made low;
> the uneven ground shall become level,
> and the rough places a plain.
> Then the glory of the Lord shall be revealed.
> and all people shall see it together,
> for the mouth of the Lord has spoken."
>   Isaiah 40:3–5

Yesterday we explored the terrain of our interior being, the terrain of our hearts: the darkness, the light, the hills, the valleys, the mountains, the dry and barren spaces. All this terrain composes the fertile-rich soil ready to receive God's whispering Word. This is the heart terrain ready to yield a rich harvest for God. It is here in the current terrain of the heart that the Advent journey begins as God whispers.

Today, spend some time practicing *lectio divina*, or divine reading. This ancient way of praying the scriptures allows the Word of God to slowly seep into the nooks and crannies of the soul, massaging the bruised places and anointing them with the salve of God's healing mercy and dancing delight in the joy-filled rooms of our heart.

Please read the full instructions on *lectio divina* before beginning your prayer experience. To practice *lectio divina* you will be reading Isaiah 40:3–5 three times. Take your time in reading. Don't rush through the words just because they have become familiar. It is most helpful if you are able to read the text out loud each time. After each reading, pause for silent reflection and open your heart and mind to God's whispers.

1. *The first reading.* After this reading, ask yourself, "What word or phrase catches my attention from this text?" This is asking for a specific phrase from the text, not something in the text that makes you think of something else … like remembering Aunt Suzie's great travel adventure through the mountains. As you pray with

this word, whispered from God, ruminate on the word in prayerful silence for ten minutes, letting it soak into your heart.

2. *The second reading.* After this reading, ask yourself, "Where does this text intersect my life?" Because the Word of God touches each moment of our lives, this question is asking you to contemplate, "Where in my experience does this text touch my life?" Does this text have a word for a relationship, situation, thought, struggle, or joy in your current life experience? As you sit in contemplation responding to the question of intersection between your life and the text, your response is likely to be longer than one simple word. Take time to let your imagination enjoy this text. Notice how God's living word is crossing your life's path. This may or may not be the same phrase from scripture with which you prayed during the first step of this prayer. Spend ten minutes in contemplative prayer as you respond to this query.

3. *The third reading.* Remember, all of God's printed word *is* a living word. It is much more than just a historical word. God's word is creating new possibility. It brings energy to life, offering what is most needed and desired. This may be a word of comfort, a felt sense of hope, peace, courage, or simply stillness by surrendering a life situation for resting in God. The creative and felt ways of God's intersection with human life are limitless. The question to contemplate after the third reading is: "What is God's invitation to me from this text?"

⤳ *Your Mandala: Listening Beyond Words for the Power of a Divine Whisper*

At the conclusion of your experience of *lectio divina*, please gather your tools of illumination: journal, pen, sketch pad, and colored pencils. Come into God's presence and settle yourself into your sacred space. Upon your sketch pad prayerfully draw your sacred circle for the creation of your mandala for today. As you gaze at the beauty of the empty space, ponder God's possibilities.

⊕ Pause. Center yourself by breathing deeply of God's infilling Spirit, letting go of all resistances and negativity within your heart.

- ⊕ Consider: How has God whispered to your heart during this prayer time as you create your mandala?
- ⊕ Let the colors of your spirit flow into the mandala as you begin to draw, considering:
  - ❖ How does the invitation you have heard from the Word of God affect the topography of your heart, both below the surface and in external actions?
  - ❖ What hope is planted within you from this prayer experience?
  - ❖ If anticipation has arisen in your spirit, by the union with God through this scripture, what does this anticipation look like, feel like, and create within you?
- ⊕ As you let the Word of God write your reflection in the drawing of your mandala, ponder the hope of Advent's dawning.
  - ❖ Prayerfully choose what colors you are drawn to.
  - ❖ Consider abstract expression, concrete images, or a mixture of both in the creation of your mandala.
  - ❖ How does the choice of colors reflect your choices on the spiritual path at this stage of your Advent *advent*ure?

I encourage you to strive to create a mandala for each daily reflection. This pictorial journey of reflection beyond words will awaken new possibility through God's wooing whispers as you listen for the advent of God's call this holy season.

Sit back and receive the anointing as the dawning of God's new birth becomes reality in your life. Enjoy the creative expression of God. If creating a mandala for today fails to inspire your heart, consider writing a journal entry, poem, or prayer to express the interior experience of *lectio divina* with the text from the prophet Isaiah.

Upon completion of your mandala, offer a silent prayer of gratitude to God for this time of prayer and interior formation of God's Spirit shaping your heart. You may want to include thanksgiving for the mystery of how God's Word shapes life and our perspective on events and people we encounter.

Ready to Receive?

Matthew 1:18–25

Twenty-first-century technology! There are so many apps, hot spots, pixels, cable connections for instantaneous methods of transmitting information. Sending and receiving has become a way of life for the postmodern world. Even my two-year-old grandbaby knows how to retrieve what she wants, when she wants it, on the family iPad. She finds her apps, plays her music, changes the songs, and plays games. Just like my grandbaby, every user of modern technology has to prepare the techno gadget to retrieve and receive the transmittal of information.

Today's quest on our Advent journey is to discover:

- How do you usually receive a word from God?
- How ready *are* you to receive from God?

Unlike our techno gadgets, human beings do not have an on/off switch or sleep mode button on the side of the body. Yet at times I wonder if we do "turn off" our spiritual receptors or slip into "hibernation mode" when it comes to receiving wooing whispers from God. Human hibernation is often unintentional. It is something that occurs when the stressors of the day show up or the schedule of life is so jam-packed that there is hardly time for a sip of water. At other times, the human hibernation mode kicks in as one mindlessly surfs the Internet or gazes blankly at the television. Boredom may cause the weariness of sleep and hibernation to overcome our waking consciousness. These stress-ors challenge and stretch our thinking and often override our posture of being present to God and attentive toward God's powerful whisper of new life.

> God is waiting to wrap loving arms around this people who had previously snubbed their Creator.

So too God stands ready to quiet each of us with [God's] love if we earnestly desire to receive that love. In God's strength we can rebuild that which has been broken down. With God's vision we can look toward a future of new possibilities. What is God saying to you about your future? Are you open to this motivating, energizing, divine love—love that offers new life in this world and in eternity?[2]

This quote from Anne Broyles came to me as I was preparing to write this reflection. It touches on human receptivity and God's desires to transmit God's presence, energy, and love to us.

Today we pause and wonder, *Am I ready?*

As we read Matthew 1:18–25, I can only imagine how Joseph may have felt receiving the information of Mary's surprising pregnancy. We don't know many facts about Joseph. We know where he was from—Bethlehem. He was a descendant from the lineage of Abraham and David, so we may have an indication of his faith and righteous posture before God. He faithfully longed to be compassionate toward Mary. He even devised a plan to care for the indiscretion of her pregnancy.

Now the birth of Jesus the Messiah took place in this way. When his mother Mary had been engaged to Joseph, but before they lived together, she was found to be with child from the Holy Spirit. Her husband Joseph, being a righteous man and unwilling to expose her to public disgrace, planned to dismiss her quietly. But just when he had resolved to do this, an angel of the Lord appeared to him in a dream and said, "Joseph, son of David, do not be afraid to take Mary as your wife, for the child conceived in her is from the Holy Spirit. She will bear a son, and you are to name him Jesus, for he will save his people from their sins." All this took place to fulfill what had been spoken by the Lord through the prophet:

"Look, the virgin shall conceive and bear a son,
and they shall name him Emmanuel,"
which means, "God is with us."

When Joseph awoke from sleep, he did as the angel of the Lord commanded him; he took her as his wife, but had no marital relations with her until she had borne a son; and he named him Jesus.

Matthew 1:18–25

I wonder:

- ◉ Were dreams a usual way for Joseph to receive the whisper of God's energizing Word?
- ◉ Was this dream so different from his "normal" and "routine" ways of discerning God's Word that it jarred him into a new plan of action?
- ◉ Could it be that Joseph walked so closely with God, that he was so practiced in noticing the nudging of God beyond the words of God's Word, that the dream was simply one of the many ways Joseph heard, listened to, trusted, and then acted upon God's love song?
- ◉ Just what did Joseph do to cause his inward being to be so ready to receive this dream call into God-action?

⌦ Your Mandala: Listening Beyond Words for the Power of a Divine Whisper

As you ponder these questions, the scripture, and the reading from today, gather your tools of illumination: journal, pen, sketch pad, and colored pencils. Come into God's presence and settle yourself into your sacred space. Upon your sketch pad prayerfully draw your sacred circle for the creation of your mandala for today. As you gaze at the beauty of the empty space, ponder God's possibilities.

- ◉ Pause. Center yourself by breathing deeply of God's infilling Spirit, letting go of all resistances and negativity within your heart.
- ◉ Let the colors of your spirit flow into the mandala as you begin to draw, considering:
    - ✤ How do you usually receive a word from God?
    - ✤ How ready *are* you to receive from God?
- ◉ As you let the Word of God write your reflections in the drawing of your mandala, ponder the hope of Advent's dawning.
    - ✤ Prayerfully choose what colors you are drawn to.
    - ✤ Consider abstract expression, concrete images, or a mixture of both in the creation of your mandala.
    - ✤ How does the choice of colors reflect your choices on the spiritual path at this stage of your Advent *advent*ure?

I encourage you to strive to create a mandala for each daily reflection. This pictorial journey of reflection beyond words will awaken new possibility through God's wooing whispers as you listen for the advent of God's call this holy season.

Sit back and receive the anointing as the dawning of God's new birth becomes reality in your life. Enjoy the creative expression of God. If creating a mandala for today fails to inspire your heart, consider writing a journal entry, poem, or prayer to express how God whispers to you through Joseph's dream and his reception of God's Word.

Upon completion of your mandala, offer a silent prayer of gratitude for this time to listen for God's unfolding whisper in the midst of your life.

Stay Awake!

Matthew 24:37–44

For as the days of Noah were, so will be the coming of the Son of
Man. For as in those days before the flood they were eating and
drinking, marrying and giving in marriage, until the day Noah
entered the ark, and they knew nothing until the flood came and
swept them all away, so too will be the coming of the Son of Man.
Then two will be in the field; one will be taken and one will be left.
Two women will be grinding meal together; one will be taken and
one will be left. Keep awake therefore, for you do not know on
what day your Lord is coming. But understand this: if the owner of
the house had known in what part of the night the thief was coming,
he would have stayed awake and would not have let his house be
broken into. Therefore you also must be ready, for the Son of Man
is coming at an unexpected hour.

> Matthew 24:37–44

What is it to stay awake? Imagine with me the following scenarios as
folks strive to keep themselves awake:

- In school, college students often pull "all-nighters" to complete
  papers and projects, leaving them exceptionally tired, groggy,
  and slow in thought for the next day or so. Some students
  in this staying-awake condition turn to outside stimuli, such
  as drinking cup after cup of coffee to keep them moving and
  motivated.
- A parent stays awake filled with anxiety and worry, awaiting the
  newly licensed teenage driver's return home from his or her first
  solo driving trip. As the minutes tick by on the clock, the imagination can fill with all kinds of fearful and difficult thoughts.

❉ A person finds him- or herself tossing and turning, unable to settle into the restoration and peace of a good night's sleep as thoughts whirl within and the prayers are lifted to God, pleading for loved ones who may be in harm's way. Some nights even the best intentions of prayer can cause sleep to evade our minds. Pictures from the nightly news are etched upon our mind's eye, and our prayers are whispered for the devastation in war-torn parts of the world. Or the neglected and poverty-ridden children living in urban blight cause the mind to race into sleeplessness. On these nights, sleep is elusive.

❉ Young parents may find being up most nights with newborn infants a trying time. Sleeplessness can dull the senses and may heighten impatience. In this state of sleep deprivation, new parents may begin to bicker over irritable attributes that they had previously overlooked in each other. At other times, in the wee hours of the night, as the new parents gaze upon the miracle of new life and wonder dawns within the soul, they are drawn into the mystery of God, yet they find sleep still eluding them.

Any of these and more scenarios are reason for folks' sleeplessness and the scripture beckons to us to stay awake. The "keeping watch" that the Gospel of Matthew speaks of is not just about sleeplessness or pulling all-nighters. Words such as "attentiveness," "alertness," and "interior listening" come to mind when we read this scripture. The wakeful and watchful state Matthew calls to our attention is one of opening space within the heart and leaning toward God in desire, expectation, and certain hope of knowing that God does indeed act and intervene in human life.

The dawning of God's advent comes with an interior posture of listening deeply, being expectant and ready to notice something of God's energy and living Word within our personal and global lives. I have found over the course of my own spiritual journey that there are some spiritual practices that serve as beloved anchors for my soul—for a time. Then an incident may occur and these beloved and cherished practices leave my spirit parched and yearning for more. So today you are asked to venture into a new posture for prayer.

Today is about noticing the song of your soul and how God is seeking to sharpen your interior senses of holy listening and expand the sight of your mind's eye. This formation of interior sight can happen in many ways, but for today the practice of noticing the presence of God comes through experiencing nature. As you head outside, leaving the haven of your sacred space to allow the beauty of creation and the natural order of God's world to inform your interior posture, listen for God's whispers. For this nature walk you may offer this prayer or one of your own for leave-taking of your sacred space. This may feel out of rhythm with the previous devotions; if so, consider how God's surprises jar us from time to time out of our comfortable rhythms of life.

> *Holy One, Holy Three, Creator of earth and sky, thank you for the beauty of this safe haven, the sacred space, which has become a holy listening place for me. I continue to offer thanksgiving for your Word whispered. Now as I rise and move from here to walk out of doors, whether through nature's beauty or stepping into the urban scene, may your gaze ignite the passion of my seeing, so that I may see the tapestry of your design all around me. Grant me attentiveness, give to me your heart of alertness, so that I may be watchful, noticing the insight of your presence as you inspire my imagination through this time of walking. May I receive and notice an expanded view of your possibilities within my life. Amen.*

Take your time on your walk. If you feel the desire to pause and gaze at something you encounter for more than a hasty walking-by glance, give yourself permission to stand in awe of what is before you. (If it is very cold and you are not able to stand for an extended gaze at an intriguing object, consider taking a camera with you, and pray with the photograph at a later time.) Allow creation and all that is around you to soak into your mind and heart. Let the mindfulness of God's presence in prayer direct your steps and lead you on the path this day.

❧ *Your Mandala: Listening Beyond Words for the Power of a Divine Whisper*

Upon your return from your prayerful walk through the beauty of God's creation, gather your tools of illumination: journal, pen, sketch pad, and colored pencils. Come into God's presence and settle yourself into your sacred space. Upon your sketch pad prayerfully draw your sacred circle for the creation of your mandala for today. As you gaze at the beauty of the empty space, ponder God's possibilities.

- ⊕ Pause. Center yourself by breathing deeply of God's infilling Spirit, letting go of all resistances and negativity within your heart.
- ⊕ Let the colors of your spirit flow into the mandala as you begin to draw, considering:
  - ✦ What awe-inspiring scene caught your attention? What was it like to stand and gaze upon it with the soft, loving eyes of God's compassion?
  - ✦ How was your spirit moved and motivated by this pilgrimage walk? With the expanse of your imagination, how did a new perspective of walking give you an opportunity for even greater attentiveness and watchfulness for the coming of God's presence?
- ⊕ As you let the Word of God write your reflections in the drawing of your mandala, sit with your reflections from the walk today and consider how God invites you into a posture of staying awake, into a new posture of being alert and ready to receive the whispers of God's new birth within your life. After your time of reflection, give your heart expression to the feelings beyond the words as you create your mandala for this day:
  - ✦ Prayerfully choose what colors you are drawn to.
  - ✦ Consider abstract expression, concrete images, or a mixture of both in the creation of your mandala.
  - ✦ How does the choice of colors reflect your choices on the spiritual path at this stage of your Advent *advent*ure?

I encourage you to strive to create a mandala for each daily reflection. This pictorial journey of reflection beyond words will awaken new possibility through God's wooing whispers as you listen for the advent of God's call this holy season.

Sit back and receive the anointing as the dawning of God's new birth becomes reality in your life. Enjoy the creative expression of God.

If creating a mandala for today fails to inspire your heart, consider writing a journal entry, poem, or prayer to express your experience of God on your walk.

After the completion of your mandala, offer a silent prayer of gratitude for this time of conversation with God. Celebrate this opportunity for reflection and intentional attentiveness to God's whispered Word.

Saturday Sabbath

This week you have taken time to intentionally notice the landscape of your heart. Through the gentle gaze of God's love you have looked beyond the surface to notice the interior shifting of inward thoughts and attitudes. Celebrate your faithfulness in coming this far on your Advent daily retreat and devotional journey! This day is your day to rest in the heart of God. You may choose simply to be consciously aware of God's presence today without further devotional reading and mandala creation, if that is what you believe God is inviting you to do.

Another option for today could be to review your mandala creations for the week. This review could take many forms. It could be placing words directly onto your creations. Or it may be spending time journaling about your week's prayer experience. This could involve looking through your pictorial journal and writing about each mandala, excavating further into your devotional times and the remembrance of God's presence and power in each daily prayer session. You may ignite your soul's passion by writing a few thoughts as an overview to how you have experienced God this week. What whispers have you heard from God this week?

If none of these options entices your spirit, you may desire to explore on your own another icon-gazing prayer experience. More illuminations from the Saint John's Bible may be found at www.saintjohnsbible.org. Or perhaps you may enjoy gazing lovingly at one of my favorite icons. The icon Virgin Orans written by Theotokos of Yaroslavl is meaningful to me, especially during this season of the year. This fifteenth-century painting of the pregnant Mary captured my heart the first time I saw it. Each year as I gaze upon it, I am drawn into the image of God present within the icon, and my heart expands in preparation for the new birthing of Jesus. If you type "Virgin Orans" into your search engine, several selections of this icon will appear for your choosing. Or if you do not have Internet access, your local library likely has works of art for further icon-gazing prayers.

 ## *Practicing Icon Gazing*

Plan at least thirty minutes for this prayer practice.

To begin, sit comfortably, and focus your eyes and heart upon the icon. Take a few deep cleansing breaths as you sit quietly, preparing to gaze at your icon. Breathe in slowly, drawing the Spirit of God into your awareness. Let God's Spirit fill your lungs with the creative possibility of God's vision. Slowly exhale all resistance and busyness from your day, leaving space for God to fill your heart and imagination.

As you wait in this space, expanding the emptiness and openness within you before God, invite God to speak to you through your chosen work of art. Trust that God's Word is creatively written in this illumination of God's whisper to speak directly to your heart.

To assist in this gazing prayer, you may wonder:

- ⊕ How does God invite you into this picture?
- ⊕ What is it about this icon that draws your heart's attention?
- ⊕ How do you imagine this noticing could be God's voice whispering a wooing love song to your heart?
- ⊕ What is God saying to you through this work of art?
- ⊕ How have you experienced the hope and anticipation this week of Jesus' Christmas birthing?
- ⊕ Consider the terrain of your heart. How is God meeting you just where you are?

Rest well, my companions; rest well near the heart of God this day.

Week Two

WHISPERING SONGS OF EXPECTATION

Choice: Listening for the Transformational Whisper

And the rush of the mighty wind swept through the
heart and mind, bringing new possibility to life.

Faith formation is a process filled with intentionality and choices. One of the easiest choices for me in my first years of parenting was to claim a family tradition that I wanted to pass on to my children. The in-home Advent wreath-lighting worship celebration quickly sprang to my heart as one way to pass along faith to the next generation while providing quality and joyful family time. Some of the gems of this family tradition shifted slightly as the new generation began practicing this faith-forming ceremony, but the core of the Story and the mystery of the lighted candles continued to illumine the ordinariness of our lives. Now that I have grown children and grandchildren, the cycle of choice continues as new parents discern what to pass on to the next generation.

The circle of the Advent wreath, as with all circles (including your daily mandala), symbolizes the never-ending, everlasting eternity of God. God was and continues to be the Word that creates life (Genesis 1–2; John 1; 2 Corinthians 2:5). God was the Word of Divinity enfleshed in Jesus (John 1). God is and forever will be the unleashed power and Divine presence in the world through Jesus' resurrection, with the outpouring of Divine love and whispers of new life through the Holy Spirit (John 20; Acts 2). Each lit candle evokes this past, present, and future essence of God in the world. The lit candles symbolize the Christ-light ignited into passionate flames of love that inwardly transform the heart.

On the second Sunday of Advent two purple candles are lit—the candle of hope from week one and a second candle traditionally known to represent Jesus' virtue of love. For me, lighting this second candle is a symbol of the human desire to live as Jesus lived, to love as Jesus loved. This way of loving is intentional and filled with choices. This life-shaping love, to live as Jesus loves, puts before us daily the questions: "What would Jesus do?" "How would Jesus love?" These questions and their answers anchor our choices on the pilgrim path of faith. Sometimes these choices lead to great "aha" moments when we feel as if we leap ahead in spiritual growth and deepen our intimacy with God. During these "aha" times, we gain new insights and perspectives. We expand our understanding of how God loves within us so that we can love others with a more perfect love of God. It is at these times, with excitement of new stirrings of God's compassion, insights, and revelations, that the whispering songs of expectation stir us to act and live more like Christ.

The choice to love leads us into many subsequent choices. We're drawn into times of self-examination that require us to hold loosely the people, things, perspectives, or theologies that we deeply cherish. Wondering about the ways we love may bring us to question the way we interact with others. Love, lightly held through faith, can indeed bring us into great joy and freedom to love as Jesus loves, but it can also lead us into challenging times of spiritual growth. It is difficult to surrender human control of circumstances, relationships, or business deals and trust God in the midst of the experience. Or sometimes situations in life that are beyond our control lead us to periods of spiritual crisis. For example, a job, a cherished relationship, a physical capability wobbles, cracks, irreparably breaks, leaving us questioning the foundations of all that we know. We may lose faith in the possibilities we once thought were there for us. During this time, when we reach out for Divine comfort and guidance, we may experience absolute assurance that God is very near to our hearts. Or we may experience the other extreme: we may encounter only silence and feel abandoned or forgotten by God. When we feel abandoned or forgotten by God, we can choose to keep our faith in the fact that God is always with us even when it doesn't feel like it—thus living out the way of God's love—or we can deny our faith, choosing to believe that God really has abandoned us. The choice is ours.

During this second week of Advent, we focus on choice and the cycle of life, a cycle of both the joy-filled times and the challenging times. The spiritual life is not a linear pursuit that moves from point A to conclusion at point Z. A more appropriate description of the spiritual life is a spiral. Think about the shape of a tornado. On the spiral circles of the tornado, the energy swirls and moves from the widest cycles of the top of the tornado down the vortex to the tip of the tornado, where the energy is the strongest. So it is with the energy of God and the descent of the spiritual life in maturity and growth as one becomes more and more shaped into loving as Jesus loves. We start broadly in faith at the top of the spiral and descend through the ever-deepening cycles of faith formation between happy, joy-filled times and difficult, sad, and challenging times. All provide opportunity to be more nearly formed into God's image at the vortex or very core of life.

We have the choice to be intentional in intensifying our opportunity to love and grow in faith. I say "intentional" because if we don't make an intentional choice, we may simply float along in faith and not experience the richness of deepened and broadened intimacy with God. We may simply remain at the beginning stages of faith of our earliest years of religious experience.

The choice to love often seems easiest during the happy times of life; however, choosing to love during the most challenging times usually brings greater spiritual maturity. The most difficult times in life, when we may feel abandoned or forgotten by God, have been called "the dark night of the soul." A dark night in this sense of faith formation is a time—maybe a day, a week, months, or years—during which we are challenged by circumstance and do not have a sense of God's presence. Old ways of noticing God may no longer bear much lively faith. However, during these dark nights, God is, in fact, closer to our souls than our minds and emotions can fathom. Together we will spend time ruminating upon what happens to the landscape of our heart during these dark nights. We will explore how they provide opportunities to deepen our faith as the flame of God's living love is ignited in our heart and increases our capacity and strength of resolve for choices of lived compassion and humility. As we find our stability more and more in God, we are ever so slowly able to loosen the grip of the old and enter into life-transforming possibilities of God.

Your Companions This Week

As Mary continues her *advent*ure on the road to Bethlehem this week, we wonder how her intimate relationship with God affected her life in relation to others. Did her blessedness and favor in God's sight ever cause her despair? Could she ever have wept with loneliness, feeling isolated and alone? What choices can you imagine arose for Mary as she sought to live faithfully and embrace the growing love of God within her?

At times, seekers through the ages have come to intimacy with God in surprising and unexpected ways. For some, as circumstances of life seemed to overwhelm, the quest to connect more deeply with God, to rely more fully on God and less upon their own achievements and talents, led to great opportunity to lean more closely into the heart of God. For others, a more difficult choice arose as they faced apparent silence, which left these seekers feeling forgotten or abandoned by God. One such seeker was Saint John of the Cross, a sixteenth-century Carmelite monk who experienced times of estranged despair when he was imprisoned for his attempts to reform the church. He coined the term "the dark night of the soul" in his poem of the same name. As John lived through this time, the choice of turning away from or toward a seemingly absent God was ever present before him. When John escaped after nine months of extreme isolation and torture, he experienced the unimaginable love of God. It was this hidden presence of God that he then knew sustained him through the dark night.

Christianity acknowledges that God is present and active in all moments of life. However, for those times when we fail to be aware of God's presence, Saint John wrote of this spiritual crisis time now known as "the dark night of the soul." As we read this week, a dark night of the soul is not just a fleeting time of unawareness, but rather a time of God's deep union with the human soul, birthing within the new possibilities through the presence of the Holy Spirit to become more Christ-like. During challenging times when we feel far from God, Saint John of the Cross determined the reality is that God is closer to our heart then we can articulate. Saint John guides us to notice the reality of God's presence through both the most challenging and the most beautiful situations of life as we move forward into deepened desire to lean into Christmas love. The question is, when we experience challenging times in life, will we choose to cling to God, even if God seems silent to us or we feel abandoned by God? How have we faced challenging times in the past?

It is this week that we often read in the Gospel of Matthew how John the Baptist, Elizabeth's son, prepared the way for Jesus' coming

(Matthew 3:1–12). John, the remarkable cousin to Jesus, was impeccable in his faithful choices. He chose to let go of his own ego. As a teacher and preacher in his own right, John lived as God loves, holding lightly his own personal desires in favor of encouraging others to live as God loves. He chose to pick up the mantle of one preparing the way for the coming of the Messiah. He did his preaching on the shore of the river. Many folks from town came out to listen to him and were inwardly moved by his words. The hearers of John's message confessed their sins, repented of ways they had separated themselves from God, and they received a baptism of repentance. At that time in history the Holy Spirit of Jesus had not been released through crucifixion and resurrection, so there were no other baptisms except a baptism of repentance. This was all a way for John to make further preparations for the coming of Jesus. The prophecy from Isaiah was fulfilled by John. He was "the voice of one crying out in the wilderness, 'Prepare the way of the Lord, make his paths straight'" (Matthew 3:3). With such popularity from his preaching and baptisms, John could have gained a big ego. His pride could have puffed up his self-image. But John chose a different path of faithfulness. He chose to not boast of his own skill. He chose to bear witness to one who was coming after him, Jesus. John chose the way of humility to lift up another rather than elevate his own status. John invites us to examine the choices we make in elevating another over our own desires and pointing to the presence of God in human life.

John's first encounter with Mary was in the silent darkness of the womb, when he leapt with joy at her greeting to Elizabeth. Walking with John, we ponder if and how John experienced the life cycle of transforming wilderness of spirit known as a dark night of the soul as he wandered through the desert eating locusts and wild honey, living a life of such simplicity and single-minded focus upon God. Did he ever feel abandoned by God? Did loneliness in the wilderness ever threaten to overtake his desires? If so, how did he choose to remain faithfully seeking God's new possibilities in life? Just how did John hold fast to the everlasting gift of hope in God?

And what about John's mother, Elizabeth? We have pondered how the faith of her husband, Zechariah, may have been formed in the terrain of his heart through the years of Elizabeth's barrenness, but what about Elizabeth? What did her spiral of faith formation look like? Was her love for God so deep that she held fast to that even when the fullness of her desire for a child was denied month after painful month, year after year? Did she discover over the years of yearning for a child that the tighter she held fast to her own desires, the less she knew of God's? How often the gifts of God's new creation have been choked off by the stranglehold of good intentions, human want, and earthly limitations. Elizabeth is one who learned through the hard knocks of life to love lightly and rest securely in God as she lived firmly on a stable foundation of Jesus' greatest commanding virtue to love God, self, and others. But did she ever encounter a dark night of the soul, feeling abandoned or forgotten by God during her years of praying for a child? Next week, we will explore further her relationship with Mary, but for now we rest with Elizabeth as we open our heart to the mystery of the Divine and human choices with a non-anxious presence without controlling desire or manipulative skill.

Your Inward Journey

Just as with Saint John of the Cross, John the Baptist, and his mother, Elizabeth, we continue to consider choices that arise in the spiritual life throughout the best and worst circumstances, challenges, and delights of our life. Are you able to love as Jesus loves even through the darkest moments of life? How do you notice God's wooing whispers shaping your interior life regardless of where you are currently living on the spiral cycle of the ever-deepening spiritual journey?

This week, pause for an intentional time away from the rush of Christmas hustle and bustle to wonder about the current condition of God's formation within your heart. We all have visions, hopes, and dreams as life unfolds. We encounter amazing opportunities and experiences. Some of these experiences bring exceeding joy and delight. Others cause us pain and heartache. Consider the mysterious silences that weave through your life. Contemplate the effect of emotions if and when you have ever felt abandoned by God. By consciously noticing your past and present awareness of God's activity or God's seemingly silent periods within your life, the way is opened to reveal the future possibilities of God's desire to gently shape your inward nature to become more Christ-like.

It is through the never-ending circle of Divine whispers in life that the formation of Jesus' new birthing shifts the landscape of your heart as the *advent*ure of this Advent expands your imagination and strengthens resolve of faithful choices. It is in the constant power and energy of God through the Holy Spirit anointing your life that Jesus' new birth is anticipated this Advent season. How will you choose to release pains from the dark night? Will you surrender so that God can provide new insight to Divine love living and working through your life as you love others?

May God's mystery of intimate grace and immeasurable knowing encircle your heart as you descend the spiral of spiritual growth into the gifts of God this week.

THE SECOND SUNDAY OF ADVENT: A CREATIVE ARTS PRAYER PRACTICE

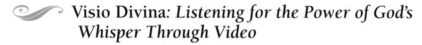 ## Visio Divina: *Listening for the Power of God's Whisper Through Video*

It *is* a wonderful life, the life we live!

We each make a holy pilgrimage—the pilgrimage of our lives. We have visions, hopes, and dreams in our heart as life unfolds, all of which give us the power of choice. No one makes this holy pilgrimage of life in isolation. We encounter many folks, from the most intimate of relationships to the chance encounter with a stranger. With each day we are gifted with numerous possibilities of success, happiness, and feelings of great fulfillment, as well as possibilities that turn to disappointment, sorrow, regrets, and grief. All make up the fabric of our life's tapestry.

Some choices bring great freedom of energy, love, and excitement and draw us closer to God. God has gifted humanity with free will. This freedom of choice is present to and for us in all situations and relationships. We experience healthy and holistic living when there is congruency between human desire to live God's love and God's will and desire, as we grow even more intentionally into that likeness of Christ. On other occasions it may seem as if we are backed into a corner with no way out. It is during these difficult circumstances of life when feelings of defeat and hopelessness arise. For some, the stress of chaos and unknowing invites us to rely with more intentionality upon the mystery of God's growing grace. Others of us may be prone to make excuses during emotionally stretching and trying seasons of life. Excuses in the fast hustle-and-bustle on the life pilgrimage often drown out the gentle whispers of God's powerful, creative hope.

Sometimes we encounter relationships or situations that are so difficult it seems as if there is no positive solution to the dilemma at hand. It is in these most heart-wrenching times on life's journey that the soul can feel far from God, stifled, as if there are no other choices. In my training to become a certified life coach, the instructor described this paralyzing position as "limiting leaps." This is when we let circumstances of life overwhelm us and we don't feel like we can make a choice in any direction.

What is a leap in life? Have you ever experienced an "aha" moment when you knew in an instant there was a new perspective, a new thought, a new breakthrough in understanding? This in-breaking or epiphany changes your outlook on life in that moment. There is no going back to old behavior after such an epiphany of "aha"! This is the hope of the in-breaking of Jesus' Holy Spirit upon us at Christmas— that it is so powerful and permanent that we are completely changed.

Leaps come upon us with an instant new perspective on something we have experienced before. Leaps can also be created by the courageous intentionality of faith as we move deeper into the cycle of Advent. This is what courage is about, empowered by the Divine whisper of God. Like the courage of Mary, we trust in God's presence and power. Courage says "yes" to God's new possibility.

When we limit the possibilities and power of God's Word, fear and resistance to the point of paralysis can set in. This tunnel vision leads to the inability to see the entire range of options and does indeed limit the leaps of God's possibility in our life. These often unconscious or emotional entrapments may cause us to feel hopeless, to give up on the situation, the relationship, or, possibly, even life itself. Yet even in the midst of such dire circumstance, God longs to whisper a powerful transforming and life-empowering Word.

How we choose to react—and with what attitude—affects the fullness of our life's journey. Consider this week: What choices have you made that affect the interior posture of your heart and soul as you transition through the shifting tides and seasons of life? What *is* the landscape of your heart currently? Has your soul become paralyzed or entrapped by limited leaps? Is your soul soaring to new heights upon God's gracious joy and limitless possibilities? Or are you somewhere in between?

To assist in our discovery of this interior posture we turn to pop culture. In 1945 *It's a Wonderful Life*, the now classic and beloved Christmas tale of a life adventure filled with choices, hopes, fears, regret, overflowing joy, and the compassion of Christ, was a box office flop! The film features James Stewart as George Bailey, who, as his life unfolds, finds himself in a fear-filled and dire circumstance from which he sees there is no way out except to end his life. Truly he is experiencing his dark night of the soul and struggling with healthy life choices. But, in the scene that particularly captivates my heart, George, at the end of all hope, after having seen what life for his loved ones would have been like had he never been born, finds the courage of heart to call out to God. The prayer he cries out is "I want to live. I want to live again." This is a life-transforming leap for George. It is this choice of intentionality and turning back to his most authentic self and embracing the advent of God's new birth that propels George into greatest joy.[1]

The advent of God's powerful Divine Word is about healing bad habits, forgiving, loving beyond limitation, and encouraging the choice of transforming leaps in life. Jesus knew how joyous and how very difficult life can be. He speaks of the depth of human emotion in a simple parable of two brothers and a father (Luke 15). The story of the prodigal son, or the forgiving father, depicts the choice of the younger brother, after carelessly spending all of his inheritance, to return to his truest God's self as he seeks forgiveness and is embraced by the father. This parable shows the joyous celebrative possibilities of God's Incarnated Word coming among us to open entrapments and to unleash the limited leaps in life. The elder brother is not at all happy about the warm acceptance given his errant brother and refuses to go to the father's welcome-home party. The elder brother, like the younger brother and the father, also has choices to make. The story ends with the elder sibling standing on the porch, refusing to go, leaving us to wonder if he chooses to join the celebration. The choice to expand our faith is always ours.

For the creative arts prayer practice this week, you will practice *visio divina*, a form of prayer much like *lectio divina*, but instead of scripture you will use a video to listen for the whispers of God. You will pray with a video depiction of the prodigal son parable from the Gospel of Luke. Through viewing this video you will have the opportunity to notice which of the three characters resonates most closely to your own heart. Could it be the moment of "coming to one's self" as the younger son, who demanded his inheritance from his father so he could live his wildest dreams, returns to his father? Or you may be drawn to the compelling and persistent love of the father. Possibly your heart will be captured by the elder son's anger, resistance, and indecision. This story has far-reaching effects because we all have the potential to be each of these characters. Within each character are the potential "aha" moments of life and the paralysis of a limited leap. Yet through it all reverberates the power of God's whispering Word, claiming for humanity how wonderful the life is that we live!

The Challenges of *Visio Divina*

One difficulty that often rears its power, particularly if you are new to *visio divina*, is getting caught up in the video story and forgetting to keep in your mind the question of how God could be whispering new insights to your heart. To help overcome this challenge, it is important to view the entire video first, simply watching for the information of the video. Notice the storyline of the video during this first viewing. After this initial viewing you will no longer be curious about the plot and outcome of the movie, so that you may focus your attention upon discerning how God's Word is speaking to you through the video.

Below I suggest a short video that I've found powerful for *visio divina*. If you would like to select your own video, though, here are a few things to keep in mind. For the prayer practice of *visio divina*, it is important to select only a short segment of video for your prayer. This could be as short as two lines from the dialogue, if that is what your heart is drawn to, but no more than a two- to three-minute segment, or else the essence of the segment gets lost in the mind and you again get caught up in the storyline. The more focused the clip for prayerful viewing, the more focused your heart can be upon God. The question of what short segment of the video to view comes into focus as you begin this prayer.

Is there a segment of the movie that inspired your heart's attention more so than other places within the video? If so, that may be a starting place to begin praying with a segment of the movie. If nothing immediately jumps out to your soul's attention, then view the video again, if the movie is short, and ask God to pierce your heart's attention with the segment of video that God would most like to speak to you with. And sometimes, as with the prodigal son video, you may want to ask questions regarding the entire short video. For example: Which character are you most like in this moment of your life? How are you like that person? Then challenge yourself to imagine how God could be expanding your compassion for others by examining a character that is opposite or different from your current attitude. Maybe if you are not satisfied in life at the moment and feel you may be coming to an "aha" choice of the younger son, imagine how the elder son could feel resentment and not want to come to your homecoming.

The final challenge of *visio divina* is time. It takes time to intentionally sit with a segment of a video asking God to whisper to your heart. As with *lectio divina*, you will play the video segment three prayerful times. With an initial viewing to get the full storyline, you will watch the video four times. Having a device for viewing that easily rewinds and has a minute counter on it is very helpful for smooth transitions between viewings.

An important dynamic of *visio divina* is to expect to encounter the living Word of God through the ordinary means of technology. God's Word is whispered to us through human voice, song, scripture, silence, picture, images, and many other ways. We are not making the image into God, but using the video image as a vehicle to hear God's voice.

Practicing *Visio Divina*

Plan at least thirty minutes for this prayer practice.

On this second Sunday of Advent, one suggestion of a video for your prayerful viewing could be the parable of the prodigal son.[2] If you do not have a computer to access a version of the prodigal son parable, you may want to rent the movie *It's a Wonderful Life* and view the bridge scene mentioned above for this exercise. However, if neither of those options is available to you, you may choose to view any video that captures your heart's attention. If the video is a major motion picture or lengthy in duration, please choose a short two- to three-minute segment of the video. If you do not have computer access, there is no problem. Do you watch television? Do you have a DVD or Blu-ray player? Any video or television show can be viewed and prayed with *visio divina*. Television shows are a little more difficult to utilize unless you can pause and rewind the show easily. Some may even want to watch a portion of a show on the small screen of their smartphone!

For an enhanced online option of *visio divina*, you may desire to pray with the video that caught my heart. The prodigal son story can be accessed on YouTube simply by typing the topic "prodigal son church film festival" or the following link into your browser: www.youtube.com/watch?v=nxfdChYCKYA. You may recall from week one the reflection piece that invited you into the ancient practice of *lectio divina*. This same prayer technique will be used while viewing and praying with a video. You will need your computer for viewing, spacious time for silent reflection, and your tools of expression for reflection. Please read the full instructions for *visio divina* before beginning your prayer experience.

1. *The first viewing.* After viewing your selected video, pause the clip and move to your sacred space for reflection, or if you are already in that space, have a sheet of paper ready to cover the computer screen so as not to be distracted. Consider: What scene from this video caught your heart's attention?

2. *The second viewing.* After viewing, pause the video and move to your sacred space for reflection, or if you are already in that space, have a sheet of paper ready to cover the computer screen so as not to be distracted. Consider: What portion of this video clip intersects with your current life? Which character are you most drawn to? Consider why you identify with this character. How do the choices of this character resonate with your heart's stirring in the Spirit of God? Does your focus character ever feel abandoned by God, paralyzed by limiting possibilities? Have you ever, like your character, gone through a similar struggle with

choice, feeling abandoned by God or overcome with the magnificent joy of homecoming?

3. *The third viewing.* After viewing, pause the video and move to
   your sacred space for reflection, or if you are already in that
   space, have a sheet of paper ready to cover the computer screen
   so as not to be distracted. Consider: What is the invitation whispered to you by God's prayer and presence through this video?
   How is God's powerful Word being whispered to your heart?
   Will this whisper lead you to an intentional choice? If so, what
   does that choice feel like, look like?

As you come into your sacred space, bringing your laptop if available
or viewing the video at the desktop, offer a prayer anointing this space.
Bring to your consciousness the possibility and expectation that in this
space you will hear God's whispers to your heart through gazing with
the soft eyes of God and listening with the inner ear of your heart. You
may use this prayer or one of your own for anointing your sacred space:

> *Holy Jesus, pour out your Spirit upon me as I view this video. Open wide*
> *my imagination, Jesus, so that my eyes may see and my ears might hear the*
> *passion of your Word whispering to my heart as I gaze upon your presence*
> *through motion picture. Help me to notice if I have limited leaps within my*
> *life and which portions of this video speak best to my experience. Help me*
> *to discern why my soul is captured by certain parts of this video. Grant me*
> *the courage to discover your invitation for my current living. I trust you,*
> *Lord, for the gifts and guidance on my pilgrimage of heart this day. Amen.*

To begin, sit comfortably, and focus your eyes and heart upon your viewing screen. Breathe in slowly, drawing the Spirit of God into your awareness. Let God's Spirit fill your lungs with the creative possibility of God's
vision. Slowly exhale all resistance and busyness from your day, leaving
space for God to fill your heart and imagination. Release any indifference
or resistance within you, allowing your heart to experience the allure of
God's love drawing you into the video. Remember Blaise Pascal's image
from this book's introduction that all humans are created with a God-
shaped emptiness within us that only God can fill, so releasing resistances
and busyness assists in making the heart ready to receive God.

As you wait in this space, expanding the emptiness and openness within you before God, invite God to speak to you through your chosen video. Trust that God's Word is creatively present in order to speak directly to your heart.

To assist in this *visio divina* prayer, I have provided a few thoughtful questions to stir the imagination and expand awareness of God's presence.

- ⊕ What is it about this video that draws your heart's attention?
- ⊕ How do you imagine what you are most attracted to in this video could be God's voice whispering a wooing love song to your heart?
- ⊕ What is God saying to you through this video?
- ⊕ How could these images lead you into your Advent discernment and discovery? Is there a choice you are facing? Are you limiting leaps within your life? Could it be that you are in a circumstance that leaves you only noticing the silence of God or feeling abandoned by God? How will you be assured that God is closer than words can describe to your heart?

 ## *Your Mandala: Listening Beyond Words for the Power of a Divine Whisper*

The creation of your mandala is the daily retreat throughout this devotional book. It takes intentional time, focus, and prayer to allow God to silence all distractions of heart and create your mandala. From your video-viewing prayer exercise, consider the landscape of your heart. How has this season of Advent affected your spiritual life and begun shaping your current thoughts and wordless wonders that your spirit may not yet be aware of? No need to try to articulate these wordless insights of God's powerful whisper; simply creating marks and colors on the page can give them expression. I invite you to draw your empty mandala circle as a symbol of the God-shaped emptiness within your soul yearning to experience Jesus' new Christmas love. As you fill the circle with colorful expression, you continue on your spiral of descent to the vortex to the new energy-shaping love of God on your Advent journey. You will focus on the choice and how these choices affect the terrain of your heart all this second week as you notice the silent mysterious ways of God. By the end of this Advent retreat you will have created a pictorial journal providing God's wordless whisper and power to you at this time in your life as you celebrate Jesus' birth at Christmas.

Gather your tools of illumination: journal, pen, sketch pad, and colored pencils. Come into God's presence and settle yourself into your sacred space. After your time of *visio divina*, take your sketch pad and prayerfully draw your sacred circle for the creation of your mandala for today. As you gaze at the beauty of the empty space, ponder God's possibilities. Let the colors of your spirit wash over the circle of your mandala.

- ⊕ As you begin the creation of your mandala, you may choose to consider:
  - ❖ What color represents the feeling of your spirit after watching this video?
  - ❖ How has this video inspired your spirit?
  - ❖ How did you notice the shimmering of God's illumination?
  - ❖ What sensations, thoughts, energies, emotions arise within you as you notice the dawning of God's presence and invitation to you through this video segment?
  - ❖ What colors best express these energies and emotions of choice, limiting leaps, or paralysis of spirit, or feelings of being abandoned by God during your dark-night experience?
  - ❖ As you let the Word of God write your reflections in the drawing of your mandala, consider abstract expression, concrete images, or a mixture of both in the creation of your mandala.

Pause here to create your mandala, expressing the felt sense of God's prayer and presence that you experienced while viewing the video of your choosing.

When you have completed your prayerful video viewing and the creation of your mandala, offer a mental prayer of thanksgiving to God for new insights and wonders that have crossed your mind during this prayer and the experience of creating your mandala.

From Generation ...
Through Generation

Matthew 1:1–17

What keeps us alive, what allows us to endure?
I think it is the hope of loving,
or being loved.
I heard a fable once about the sun going on a journey
to find its source, and how the moon wept
without her lover's
warm gaze.
We weep when light does not reach our hearts. We wither
like fields if someone close
does not rain their
kindness
upon
us.[3]

> Meister Eckhart, "The Hope of Loving"

Meister Eckhart's poem rings as true in the twenty-first century as it did in the thirteenth century. Finding our source is the quest of the faith journey. Finding the source of God is the goal of the seeking heart's journey to live more and more into that image of Divine love. The poem states, "The sun going on a journey to find its source...." How natural it is to desire to know the source and origin of one's life. We have a yearning from within to know from where we came, to discover union with God through the generations. For some, this may take the form of family lineage; others may know mentorship and faith forma-tion best through spiritual kinships. Spiritual kinships are relationships in which people have been nurtured, raised, and mentored in faith in such a loving way that they become like family. Today we are faced with the choice of looking in the rearview mirror to consider from where we came. Will it be difficult to look back? Will it bring great joy? Are you willing to be courageous and make the choice of awareness, to know how your heart is shaped by your spiritual lineage?

Meister Eckhart knew well the yearning of the heart *from* one generation to the next. It became for him sacramental as God's love went *through* one generation into the next. Like Eckhart, we experience honest, open-hearted yearning for love from the source of God as the union of Divine and human is forged through the birth of Jesus. God is incarnated as Jesus. Jesus is energy, power, and Divine presence birthed in human form. Yet the tender example established by Eckhart gives voice to the passionate Incarnate Love that nearly excommunicated Eckhart from the Catholic Church!

> It was life itself that Eckhart loved to talk about: the life of the fields and the life of the sky, and the wonders of the human heart.... [He writes:] *"Is this not a holy trinity: the firmament, the earth, our bodies. And is it not an act of worship to hold a child, and till the soil and lift a cup."*[4]

Entering further into the second week of Advent leads us straight into the passionate words of Eckhart's kinship of love. Engaging the Matthean text that begins with the genealogy of Jesus, we pause to notice the formation of faith from generation through generation and the mysterious pathways of God. Each generation must themselves become the "birther" or bearer of the Holy Light of God's presence, prayer, and grace to the next generation. This is the way faith traditions—the lighting of the Advent wreath for my family, for example—are passed down through the generations. As the Story is told, our hearts are ignited in love of God. It is through this faith sharing from generation through generation that openness and receptivity to God's power and presence within the soul are unveiled.

In the beginning of my faith *advent*ure, I was often tempted to skip over the long lists of who begot whom in the Bible. Then as my understanding of God's formation within my life deepened, I embraced the rich, fertile soil of God's love passing from generation through generation. There have been many profoundly influential people in my life, shaping my love for God. For these dear ones I am eternally and deeply grateful. Today we will take a lengthy reflective pause to gaze back upon your biological and/or spiritual lineage.

An account of the genealogy of Jesus the Messiah, the son of David, the son of Abraham.

Abraham was the father of Isaac, and Isaac the father of Jacob, and Jacob the father of Judah and his brothers, and Judah the father of Perez and Zerah by Tamar, and Perez the father of Hezron, and Hezron the father of Aram, and Aram the father of Aminadab, and Aminadab the father of Nahshon, and Nahshon the father of Salmon, and Salmon the father of Boaz by Rahab, and Boaz the father of Obed by Ruth, and Obed the father of Jesse, and Jesse the father of King David.

And David was the father of Solomon by the wife of Uriah, and Solomon the father of Rehoboam, and Rehoboam the father of Abijah, and Abijah the father of Asaph, and Asaph the father of Jehoshaphat, and Jehoshaphat the father of Joram, and Joram the father of Uzziah, and Uzziah the father of Jotham, and Jotham the father of Ahaz, and Ahaz the father of Hezekiah, and Hezekiah the father of Manasseh, and Manasseh the father of Amos, and Amos the father of Josiah, and Josiah the father of Jechoniah and his brothers, at the time of the deportation to Babylon.

And after the deportation to Babylon: Jechoniah was the father of Salathiel, and Salathiel the father of Zerubbabel, and Zerubbabel the father of Abiud, and Abiud the father of Eliakim, and Eliakim the father of Azor, and Azor the father of Zadok, and Zadok the father of Achim, and Achim the father of Eliud, and Eliud the father of Eleazar, and Eleazar the father of Matthan, and Matthan the father of Jacob, and Jacob the father of Joseph the husband of Mary, of whom Jesus was born, who is called the Messiah.

So all the generations from Abraham to David are fourteen generations; and from David to the deportation to Babylon, fourteen generations; and from the deportation to Babylon to the Messiah, fourteen generations.

Matthew 1:1–17

Your Mandala: Listening Beyond Words for the Power of a Divine Whisper

Gather your tools of illumination: journal, pen, sketch pad, and colored pencils. Come into God's presence and settle yourself into your sacred space. Upon your sketch pad prayerfully draw your sacred circle for the creation of your mandala for today. As you gaze at the beauty of the empty space, ponder God's possibilities.

- ⊕ Pause. Center yourself by breathing deeply of God's infilling Spirit, letting go of all resistances and negativity within your heart.
- ⊕ Reread Matthew 1:1–17. Notice the number of years this lineage spans: fourteen generations three times over. Throughout these generations every human attribute and every human emotion were experienced while powerful and mystic experiences of God were known.
- ⊕ Let the colors of your spirit flow into the mandala as you begin to draw, considering:
  - ✤ Holding your biological and/or spiritual kinship lineage in your heart:
    - ❊ What colors best express your faith formational experience from generation through generation?
    - ❊ What are the striking moments of God's presence that shine brightly?
    - ❊ How would you depict your historical, biological, and/or spiritual kinship lineage? Has the path of faith formation passed through generations been a gradual ascent, wrought with pitfalls, rocky cliffs, and gorges? Has the way been steady, with little or no assistance, simply a path that God alone has led you on?
    - ❊ What choices have been made over the years that have directly or indirectly affected your current pilgrimage of faith?
    - ❊ Have there been times of great spiritual joy or instances of feeling lost or abandoned by God as silence seemed to loom larger than faith?

- ❖ How does the light of Christ's Incarnation illumine your history?
- ❖ What sensations, thoughts, energies, emotions arise within you as you pray back through your generations?
- ◉ As you let the Word of God write your reflections in the drawing of your mandala, ponder the hope of Advent's dawning.
  - ❖ Prayerfully choose what colors you are drawn to.
  - ❖ Consider abstract expression, concrete images, or a mixture of both in the creation of your mandala.
  - ❖ How does the choice of colors reflect your choices on the spiritual path at this stage of your Advent *adventure*?

I encourage you to strive to create a mandala for each daily reflection of this Advent retreat. This pictorial journey of reflection beyond words will awaken new possibility through the powerful Divine whisper as you listen for the advent of God's call this holy season.

Sit back and receive the anointing as the dawning of God's new birth becomes reality in your life. Enjoy the creative expression of God. If creating a mandala for today fails to inspire your heart, consider writing a journal entry, poem, or prayer to express your own seeking heart's journey to find the source of God.

Upon completion of your mandala, offer a silent prayer of gratitude for your history, which is the foundation upon which your faith is built. Specifically name before God those who held you in Divine love and opened and encouraged you on your passionate love affair of faith.

Darkness Descends ...

Isaiah 9:2, 6

The sixteenth-century poet, mystic, and theologian Saint John of the Cross writes of "the dark night of the soul" as a profound time of transformation and deepening relationship with God. A dark night of the soul is a time of spiritual crisis when a person feels an absence of God's presence, even as he or she may have a sense that God is very near. This sounds like double-talk—seeming absent yet being nearer than a person's senses can know—but as we'll notice today, God unravels the mystery of holiness as difficult situations and circumstance draw humans into an increasing intimacy with the Divine.

Saint John of the Cross's first experience of "the dark night of the soul" came with his first imprisonment as he literally and spiritually groped in the darkness to find his center of orientation. As John suffered in the pit of the dark prison, he felt a complete absence of God. This was not just a momentary fleeting wonder if God was real, alive, or dead. The prison was so dark John was unable to see physically with his eyes. And the heaviness of his spirit—feeling totally abandoned by God in this pit—left John in spiritual darkness. His logic said yes, God was near, but his emotions had no sense of God's presence.

A complete sense of absence of God leads you to doubt everything you have formerly believed. It leaves you wandering through life in a spiritual void, unaware of God's constant presence. This sense of not feeling God's presence in the midst of your faith journey is a hidden state of formation. This dark night of the soul can occur at any time of year and in any stage of faith. A dark night may last in duration only a short time or may continue, appearing to never end.

As the winter solstice is almost upon us in this second week of Advent, pause to notice the struggle of new spiritual birth. The labor pains that accompany the quest for birthing move you into even deeper relationship with God. Today, we pause to contemplate the labor pains of resistances and their relationship to spiritual well-being. Resistances to new spiritual insights could be in the realm of emotional, psychological, situational, or even with the dawning of awareness that a beloved prayer practice may have dried up as a source of inspiration.

In a dark night of the soul, resistances toward the very thing that you seek and love, namely a more intimate union with God, leave your heart restless and yearning for something more. The echoes of Saint Augustine's words name this deep, unspoken yearning: "Our hearts are restless until they can find rest in you."[5] Resistances to spiritual new birthing come as you hold fast to loves other than God. These loves are named as "attachments." You may become attached to prayer styles, love of children, spouse, parents, and circumstances, all of which may be good and healthy unless these attachments surpass your deepest love for God.

Jesus' question to Peter at a resurrection appearance from the Gospel of John comes to mind: "Do you love me more than these?" (John 21:15). As you pause and consider the answer to Jesus' question to Peter, the wonder unfolds. The answer might be, "No, I *want* to love you more, but sorry, Jesus, my children, my prayer style, or whatever has a greater hold in my reality than you." If so, it is time for an examination of the heart. When we love attachments, the "more than these," then the power of God's Divine whisper may be blocked from our reality. The act of letting these attachments go often leads to a descent into darkness. The realization that even your deepest and healthiest loves can create barriers to new spiritual life can cause devastating results and plunge you into deep depression or despair. Just like the energy of the spiral tornado, so the swirling descent to the vortex of experiencing God in new ways can plunge us into uncertainties and leave us feeling abandoned by God because God appears to be silent. Letting go of the need to control, affirm, and protect attachments purifies the heart and opens the way for Jesus' new birth to dawn in life.

As the depths of knowing and being known by God shift in the dark night, it is a time that draws people into renewed passionate love for God. God does not create the most challenging times simply to trip us up. God yearns to deepen human experience of God's great and amazing love for us and uses these hard times for interior formation of the heart. As the attitudes, perceptions, insights of the heart shift with the hidden presence of God during the dark night, we are freed from the restraints of our former ways of life, and God whispers, "Come into the new way of love and faith, my beloved one." The dark night can be scary as we teeter suspended between the old and the new while feeling the shift of energies within the soul. We feel the entirety of being is anointed from beyond self by God's grace.

The miracle of the dark night for Saint John of the Cross was that through this time of "not knowing" God's nearness, God was closer to his spirit than words could articulate. God held his tenacious spirit. God was nearer to John during this very difficult imprisonment than John's conscious awareness could even imagine.

A dark night of the soul is not just an experience for the saints of old who sought holy pilgrimage. You and I are invited to attend to the presence of God with the inner ear of our heart and notice the seeming absence of God or the catastrophic events drawing us into the darkness where the light of Christ may feel absent. For this daily reflection you are asked to contemplate your dark night and the choices before you during and after such a challenging time.

I remember a season through which I lived and I now affection-ately call exile. It was only a few short years, yet the leaps and bounds of God's formation within my soul were astounding. Former ways of praying fell flat and lost their appeal to my heart. Deep within me, at a soul-knowing depth of understanding, I knew beyond all reason that God was nearer to my heart than my conscious awareness could fathom. Trusting God's nearness, even in the darkness of exile, my soul learned new heights of joy in love with God and descended the spiral of faith formation to even greater depths of awe, gratefulness, rever-ence, and humility. It was there in exile that I picked up the colored pencils and began my first wordless expression of God's deep interior and powerfully life-giving whisper.

The prophet Isaiah cries out the living word of God to a people who have become lost in darkness, proclaiming the mighty healing pos-sibility of the Divine love:

The people who walked in darkness
have seen a great light;
those who lived in a land of deep darkness—
on them light has shined....
For a child has been born for us,
a son given to us;
authority rests upon his shoulders;
and he is named
Wonderful Counsellor, Mighty God,
Everlasting Father, Prince of Peace.
Isaiah 9:2, 6

Your Mandala: Listening Beyond Words for the Power of a Divine Whisper

Gather your tools of illumination: journal, pen, sketch pad, and colored pencils. Come into God's presence and settle yourself into your sacred space. Upon your sketch pad prayerfully draw your sacred circle for the creation of your mandala for today. As you gaze at the beauty of the empty space, ponder God's possibilities.

- Pause. Center yourself by breathing deeply of God's infilling Spirit, letting go of all resistances and negativity within your heart.
- Reread Isaiah 9:2, 6. It is important to keep the experience of the dark night in perspective. Trust in the prophet Isaiah. Do not let the memory or the current reality of the darkness consume your being. Make this memory a touchstone for today, leaning into the possible dawning of light through God's illumining birth as the Prince of Peace comes to you.
- Let the colors of your spirit flow into the mandala as you begin to draw, considering:
    - When in your life have you experienced or are you currently experiencing a dark night of the soul?
        - What choices can you imagine could arise for you during this challenging time?
        - What colors best express that descent into darkness or the uncertainty of indecision?

❖ How did the light of Christ's dawning love illumine your
darkness?

❖ What choices has God opened to your imagination during
this time of prayer?

❖ If you are still waiting in the darkness of the night for the
dawning of God's illumination, imagine what the dawning
of Jesus' light could feel like, look like, and sound like for
you during your challenging period of darkness.

❖ What sensations, thoughts, energies, emotions arise within
you as you notice the dawning of God's light?

⊕ As you let the Word of God write your reflections in the drawing of your mandala, ponder the hope of Advent's dawning.

❖ What colors are you drawn to?

❖ Consider abstract expression, concrete images, or a mixture of both in the creation of your mandala.

❖ How does the choice of colors reflect your choices on the
spiritual path through the most challenging times?

I encourage you to strive to create a mandala for each daily reflection.
This pictorial journey of reflection beyond words will awaken new pos-
sibility through God's wooing whispers as you listen for the advent of
God's call this holy season.

Sit back and receive the anointing as the dawning of God's new
birth becomes reality in your life. Enjoy the creative expression of God.
If creating a mandala for today fails to inspire your heart, consider writing a journal entry, poem, or prayer to express God's illumination of
your time of darkness.

Upon completion of your mandala, offer a silent prayer of release
of the darkness and gratitude for the choices present before you this
day as you continue your Advent *advent*ure into the holiness of Jesus'
new birth.

Fashioning a Heart of Love

Ezekiel 36:25–28

At this point on the Advent journey, the terrain of your heart is shifting and becoming even more pliable in the hands and heart of God than when you started this Advent *advent*ure. Hear the word from the prophet Ezekiel:

> I will sprinkle clean water on you, and you will be clean; I will cleanse you from all your impurities and from all your idols. I will give you a new heart and put a new spirit in you; I will remove from you your heart of stone and give you a heart of flesh. And I will put my Spirit in you and move you to follow my decrees and be careful to keep my laws. Then you will live in the land I gave your ancestors; you will be my people, and I will be your God.
>   Ezekiel 36:25–28 NIV

The folks to whom Ezekiel spoke have been wandering in darkness. They have lost their centeredness. That is to say, they have lost their way not just geographically but also in faith. They are aimlessly trying many and various ways to quench the thirst of their souls and yet not connecting solidly with God. With this passage from Ezekiel, God proclaims God's greatest desire. Coming like a blazing fire, roaring in the hearth on a cold winter's night, God's Word offers hope and encouragement to each longing heart.

Saint John of the Cross knew of such passionate love, both a love from and a longing for God. His most famous poem reads:

> O living flame of love
> That tenderly wounds my soul
> In its deepest center! Since
> Now you are not oppressive,

Now consummate! if it be your will:
Tear through the veil of this sweet encounter! …

O lamps of fire!
In whose splendors
The deep caverns of feeling,
Once obscure and blind,
Now give forth, so rarely, so exquisitely,
Both warmth and light to their Beloved.[6]
> Saint John of the Cross, "The Living Flame of Love"

Today's reflection is about noticing how the light of Christ's dawning love illumines your heart and makes pliable your desires and love for the expectant birth of Jesus. There are several ways to contemplate how God is fashioning your heart, molding it, shaping it into this new possibility and insight experienced as the birthing of Jesus' Divine presence:

⊛ You may want to consider creating a mandala while listening to the music video mentioned below.

⊛ You may choose to reread the Ezekiel text and ponder what is most attractive to your spirit from this text. If the text speaks to your creative spirit, you may choose to follow the form of prayer from week one for *lectio divina*.

 Your Mandala: Listening Beyond Words for the Power of a Divine Whisper

Gather your tools of illumination: journal, pen, sketch pad, and colored pencils. Come into God's presence and settle yourself into your sacred space. Upon your sketch pad prayerfully draw your sacred circle for the creation of your mandala for today. As you gaze at the beauty of the empty space, ponder God's possibilities.

⊛ Pause. Center yourself by breathing deeply of God's infilling Spirit, letting go of all resistances and negativity within your heart.

⊕ To begin your contemplative prayer this day, type into your browser www.youtube.com/watch?v=-vlcDdwINV0, where you can listen to John Michael Talbot's recording of Saint John of the Cross' "Living Flame of Love." If you do not have computer access, simply read the above verses from John of the Cross' poem "The Living Flame of Love" for your contemplation.

⊕ Let the colors of your spirit flow into the mandala as you begin to draw, considering how you will proceed with this daily prayer experience: while listening to the song with *audio divina*, viewing the video with *visio divina*, or reading aloud the poem or scripture from Ezekiel with *lectio divina*? Once you have chosen your method, discern:

 ❖ What choices arise for you from this practice?
 ❖ How will these choices open the way for you to experience greater passion and love of God?

⊕ As you let the Word of God write your reflections in the drawing of your mandala, ponder the hope of Advent's dawning.

 ❖ Prayerfully choose what colors you are drawn to.
 ❖ Consider abstract expression, concrete images, or a mixture of both in the creation of your mandala.
 ❖ How do these colors represent your new insights at this stage on your *adven*ture?

I encourage you to strive to create a mandala for each daily reflection. This pictorial journey of reflection beyond words will awaken new possibility through God's wooing whispers as you listen for the advent of God's call this holy season.

Sit back and receive the anointing as the dawning of God's new birth becomes reality in your life. Enjoy the creative expression of God. If creating a mandala for today fails to inspire your heart, consider writing a journal entry, poem, or prayer to express how coming through a dark night of the soul turns to deep hope and joy in passionate love for God.

Upon completion of your mandala, offer a silent prayer of gratitude as you continue your Advent *adven*ture into the holiness of Jesus' new birth.

The Power of a Whisper

Luke 1:5–25

> In the days of King Herod of Judea, there was a priest named
> Zechariah, who belonged to the priestly order of Abijah. His wife
> was a descendant of Aaron, and her name was Elizabeth. Both of
> them were righteous before God, living blamelessly according to
> all the commandments and regulations of the Lord. But they had
> no children, because Elizabeth was barren, and both were getting
> on in years.
>
> Luke 1:5–7

Zechariah and Elizabeth were two people who experienced the dark night
of disappointment and the passion of "the living flame of love." Imagine
the years of longing, each month leaving Elizabeth bracing herself for the
feeling that her body was betraying her deepest desire for a child. Day
in and day out as age progressed and faith matured, maybe Elizabeth saw
her passionate desire for a child as an attachment and released it as an
offering to God. Imagine the years of prayers that seemed to fall upon
deaf Divine ears. And still notice the years of Elizabeth and Zechariah's
unwavering compassion, love, and devotion to God's presence.

Both Zechariah and Elizabeth stand upon the firm foundation of
faithful ancestral heritage. Zechariah offered his life in service to God as
a priest. Out of love and devotion to God he left his beloved wife and
journeyed to Jerusalem, honored to accept the priestly duty of temple
sacrifice. Imagine how many years of faithful service he lived honoring
God with awe and reverence.

Elizabeth, too, lived a life of devotion built upon the foundation of faithful genealogy and generations of believers. The reality of
Elizabeth's life as a priest's wife may have been filled with trials and
patience, gifts and devotion. Imagine the witness she lived and shared

with her beloved cousin Mary. Elizabeth may have been one of the family members who nurtured Mary, modeling unwavering faith even through the most difficult personal and private trials of barrenness.

All it took was a word from God for Zechariah and Elizabeth's life to turn upside down and all around as they became the proud expectant parents of John. The creative Word of God's whisper became reality, enfleshed in the life of their son. Two ordinary people with a deep desire to love God were gifted with the miraculous power and presence of God's life-giving, creative whispered Word. And then it happened. The gift of listening beyond the surface was Elizabeth's as her unborn child leapt in her womb at the sight of Mary.

Your Mandala: Listening Beyond Words for the Power of a Divine Whisper

Gather your tools of illumination: journal, pen, sketch pad, and colored pencils. Come into God's presence and settle yourself into your sacred space. Upon your sketch pad prayerfully draw your sacred circle for the creation of your mandala for today. As you gaze at the beauty of the empty space, ponder God's possibilities.

- Pause. Center yourself by breathing deeply of God's infilling Spirit, letting go of all resistances and negativity within your heart.
- Slowly read Luke 1:5–25. Take time to pause throughout your reading to notice what words catch your attention and speak most directly to your heart.
- Let the colors of your spirit flow into the mandala as you begin to draw, considering:
  - The essence of the years of Elizabeth and Zechariah's long- ing, experiencing disappointment and unfulfilled dreams, and the possible surprising fulfillment of such desire.
  - Your steadfast yearning to be faithful to God even through personal heartache and struggles. What choices do you face during those times?
  - The stability of heart and soul in God as you learn from disappointment and deepen your faith. Think of the spiral

of spiritual formation cycling downward toward the heart of God. What color best represents this for you?

❖ Ponder from the scripture where and how this living Word of God intersects with your life.

❖ What is the invitation for you from this living Word of God?

❖ Are there any shifts from what has been deemed impossible to what may be possible with God?

⊕ As you let the Word of God write your reflections in the drawing of your mandala, ponder the hope of Advent's dawning.

❖ Prayerfully choose what colors you are drawn to.

❖ Consider abstract expression, concrete images, or a mixture of both in the creation of your mandala.

❖ How does the choice of colors reflect your choices on the spiritual path at this stage of your Advent *adven*ture?

I encourage you to strive to create a mandala for each daily retreat reflection. This pictorial journey of reflection beyond words will awaken new possibility through God's wooing whispers as you listen for the advent of God's call this holy season.

Sit back and receive the anointing as the dawning of God's new birth becomes reality in your life. Enjoy the creative expression of God. If creating a mandala for today fails to inspire your heart, consider writing a journal entry, poem, or prayer to express God's illumination of your time of darkness and the choices that appeared during this time. Then celebrate the encompassing love of God's unique Divine embrace during this challenging time.

Upon completion of your mandala, offer a silent prayer of gratitude and humble reverence as you continue your Advent *adven*ture into the holiness of Jesus' new birth.

Standing at the Crossroads of "Me or Thee?"

Matthew 3:1–12
Luke 3:1–18

This week began with familial history and the influence this lineage has upon your spiritual life. Looking back gives rich and fertile landscape for faith formation through spiritual kinships that have borne us up. Today with an eye and heart looking toward the future, we turn our attention to John, the son of Elizabeth and Zechariah. A cousin to Jesus, and only six months his senior, John was a great preacher who drew large crowds out from the city of Jerusalem to the Jordan River, where he baptized those who repented. So passionately did John speak of God's presence and power of repentance, as he stood bridging the old ways of relating to God and proclaiming the new, that folks wondered if he could possibly be the One for whom they had been waiting. Could John be the Christ?

John presents us with a vision of humility. He had a very intimate relationship with God, so mysteriously close that even in utero he knew the presence of God and leapt for joy. Yes, he was gifted—very gifted, in fact. (Humility is not about diminishing one's giftedness.) The crowds went out of their way to listen to him preach. They flocked to him to be baptized. He could easily have gained a swelled self-image and claimed, "What a great 'church growth' guy I am!" But with all of his preaching and all of his baptizing, John had another goal in mind. John chose the spiral of spiritual formation and moved downward toward the heart of God by his humble lifestyle.

Humility is *not* one of the most popular attributes of twenty-first-century pop culture! Very few, if any, television shows, movies, or songs have main characters that depict humility or focus on messages of humility. John Wayne mentalities of rough, rugged, and self-made persons dot the headlines as folks "rise to the top" of business, politics, and prominent leadership. The blame and shame games of relationship so prevalent in society are not based upon humility, nor do these seek to bolster anyone but the self. Even though humility is not the foundation of pop culture, it *is* a characteristic that many people strive to live.

There are many techniques that help us lean toward the inward posture of humility. John, however, takes the path of humility one step further. Humility for John was more than just keeping his own ego in check, living the fruits of the spirit, and relying on his innate sense of God's guidance, presence, and Word. John's entire message was pointing toward the gifts and qualities of another. His whole focus was on elevating another above himself. John had the ability to know the inward gifts and graces of his cousin. John went before Jesus, preparing the hearts and minds of others so that the folks would be ready to hear and receive Jesus' new way of relationship with God. John stands at a crossroads between the old theology and faith practices and the new way of Jesus. The totality of John's life and ministry focused on the descending way of humility. This new way of relating to God comes through the birth, death, and resurrection of Jesus. Consider:

- ⊕ Do I intentionally seek the giftedness of others and elevate them above myself?
- ⊕ How do I open the way for others to be ready to receive the word and presence of Jesus? What habits, practices, attitudes, and mannerisms must I pick up and what must I lay down to live humility? This question is not just about preaching, teaching, or public witness and professions of faith. The question is deep beyond the surface. It leans into the wonder of the inward being.
- ⊕ In this process of becoming more humble, who is it that I am elevating above myself, not because of age, rank, or position, but because I see with my mind's eye the beauty of another's soul and yearn to encourage the bursting forth of this person's gifts rather than my own?
- ⊕ Humility is looking forward and seeing the Divine presence in the other and calling it forth.

Your Mandala: Listening Beyond Words for the Power of a Divine Whisper

Gather your tools of illumination: journal, pen, sketch pad, and colored pencils. Come into God's presence and settle yourself into your sacred space. Upon your sketch pad prayerfully draw your sacred circle for the creation of your mandala for today. As you gaze at the beauty of the empty space, ponder God's possibilities.

- ⊕ Pause. Center yourself by breathing deeply of God's infilling Spirit, letting go of all resistances and negativity within your heart.
- ⊕ Take an extended time to pray with John the Baptist this day. Read Matthew 3:1–12 and Luke 3:1–18. These texts have similarities and lift up different information about John.
- ⊕ Let the colors of your spirit flow into the mandala as you begin to draw, considering:
  - ✤ Who is it that you seek to elevate beyond yourself?
  - ✤ How do you or will you intentionally encourage the giftedness of others to shine brightly?
  - ✤ The roles that we live and work—such as teaching, preaching, and proclaiming—present the outward appearance of a person. Through these roles, how do you focus priority on helping others be ready for the coming of Jesus?
  - ✤ What choices do you struggle with as you encourage another while at the same time diminishing your own power?
  - ✤ Draw a mandala expressing your humility. What choices come before you if you are to live humility with sincerity?
- ⊕ As you let the Word of God write your reflections in the drawing of your mandala, ponder the hope of Advent's dawning.
  - ✤ What colors are you drawn to?
  - ✤ Consider abstract expression, concrete images, or a mixture of both in the creation of your mandala.
  - ✤ How does the choice of colors reflect your choices on the spiritual path at this stage of your Advent *advent*ure?

I encourage you to strive to create a mandala for each daily retreat reflection. This pictorial journey of reflection beyond words will awaken new possibility through God's wooing whispers as you listen for the advent of God's call this holy season.

Sit back and receive the anointing as the dawning of God's new birth becomes reality in your life. Enjoy the creative expression of God. If creating a mandala for today fails to inspire your heart, consider writing a journal entry, poem, or prayer to express God's illumination of the choices you live to follow the pathway of humility.

Upon completion of your mandala, offer a silent prayer asking to increase humility, to obtain courage to live the choice of humility, and to gain sight to see the presence of Christ in others as you continue your journey to the manger.

Saturday Sabbath

This day is your day to rest in the heart of God. You may choose simply to breathe God's Spirit today by having a quiet day of retreat without further devotional reading and mandala creation.

Another option for today could be to review your mandala creations for the week. As you review your mandalas, consider how God is gifting you with the freedom of choice. Have you struggled this week with a spiritual crisis from a dark night of the soul? Are there folks within your spiritual kinship who encourage you to leap beyond your self-imposed limitations on what is truly possible with God? Which one of the cast of characters accompanying you this week from the daily readings spoke most directly to your heart? As you conclude this week, what would you name as your greatest insight for new growth and shaping of Jesus' virtue of love? How can you imagine that you will cling to this gift of love from the Advent's candle-lighting wisdom and share it with others?

This review of your mandalas can take many forms. You could place words directly onto your creations. This would assist in articulating and remembering what each picture is at its core essence. Or you may spend intentional time journaling about your week's prayer experience. You could review the week by creating a mandala from the insights that you gained in looking at the daily mandalas that you have created. Or you may ignite your soul's passion by writing a few thoughts as an overview to how you have experienced God this week.

What whispers have you heard from God this week?

If none of these options entices your spirit, you may desire to explore on your own one more *visio divina* prayer experience. To practice *visio divina* you may use any video clip or a portion of a movie. You will follow the same instructions found on pages 46 to 49. I offer new reflection questions based on this week's practices below. The content of the video should be something that is attractive to your soul. Perhaps it is an animated show, a popular major motion picture—even home movies on your cell phone can become the inspiration for this prayerful *visio divina*. A plethora of choices, from original videos to clips to your favorite major motion pictures, can be found on YouTube. If you choose to pray with a portion of a major motion picture, remember that only a two- to three-minute segment of the movie is necessary. As you recall from your first day of this week, the creative arts experience of praying with the video depiction of the prodigal son parable, you will view the same video or segment of a video four times. With each viewing you will focus on questions from the prayer practice of *visio divina*.

⟳ *Practicing* Visio Divina

Plan at least thirty minutes for this practice. Prayerfully consider what video you would like to pray with.

As you wait in this space, expanding the emptiness and openness within you before God, invite God to speak to you through your chosen video. Trust that God's Word is creatively alive even through video, to speak directly to your heart.

1. *The first viewing.* After viewing your selected video, pause the clip and move to your sacred space for reflection, or if you are already in that space, have a sheet of paper ready to cover the computer screen so as not to be distracted. Consider: What scene from this video caught your heart's attention? Why?

2. *The second viewing.* After viewing, pause the video and move to your sacred space for reflection, or if you are already in that space, have a sheet of paper ready to cover the computer screen so as not to be distracted. Consider: What portion of this video intersects with your current life? Are there choices to be made? Have you experienced limited leaps of spiritual insight? Are you bogged down in darkness, awaiting the illumination of God's light?

3. *The third viewing.* After viewing, pause the video and move to your sacred space for reflection, or if you are already in that space, have a sheet of paper ready to cover the computer screen

so as not to be distracted. Consider: What is the invitation whispered to you by God's prayer and presence through this video? How is God's powerful Word being whispered to your heart?

Upon completion of your *visio divina* prayer, pause with your mandala and examine your heart to name what choices have arisen before you on your descending spiral of faith and humility through this process of *visio divina*.

When you have concluded your time of weekly reflection and Sabbath rest, you may pray this prayer or one of your own, offering thanksgiving for beautiful insights into God's new hope and love arising within you this Advent season:

> *Holy and generous God, I thank you for this time of prayer. You have opened my eyes, expanded my heart, and granted me your abiding presence as you whispered to my soul from this video. May the words of your heart continue to bring the good news of your power and presence into my life as I step ever more closely to your new birth. Let the dawn of your advent bring new possibility as I walk through these holy days of preparation and expectation. Amen.*

Rest well, my dear companions; rest near the heart of God.

Week Three

Companions for the Journey

Deep Joy: Listening to the Soul's Song

What is that feeling? What is that tug at my heart?
Could it be God's design coming into my life?

It was a long car ride. My three-year-old granddaughter in the back seat had just finished a day of preschool and she was hungry. It saddened me, knowing there was nothing for her to eat in the car. Hoping to distract her from her hunger, I suggested that next week on our drive home maybe we could plan to stop and get something to eat, or maybe we could bring a peanut butter and jelly sandwich to satisfy her hunger. It was then my heart melted at the sounds of her words. "Oh, Amma, I love you! Would you really do that for me?" Her circumstances had not changed, her hunger was still there, but the promise of hope shifted the terrain of her heart and caused spontaneous joy and love to burst forth with gratefulness and thanksgiving.

Spontaneous joy! The third week of Advent celebrates soul-deep joy. This third week of Advent the pink candle is lit—the candle of joy. In some traditions this candle is referred to as Mary's candle. After the angel Gabriel's conversation with Mary, I can imagine Mary's life could have been one of surprises, difficult decisions, and hard conversations with Joseph, her family, neighbors, and friends. Even with difficult conversations and surprising moments of life, Mary lived from a soul-deep reliance upon the promise of God to satisfy the hunger of new life growing within her. It is this soul-deep reliance upon God, and con-sistently looking for God's presence in life, that brought her great joy even when life circumstances held tensions and struggle. For me, this is the week that Mary models the need for intentional retreating and spiritual companionship with soul-deep listening to the inward groaning of the spirit as we approach Jesus' birthing season of Christmas.

The annual rhythm of lighting the Advent wreath anchors fam-ily and church life alike in soul-deep joy as we experience the cosmic

Divine whisper of love. The Advent or "in-breaking" of God's indwelling in humanity unties our memories of the past, helps us hold lightly the present, and turns our gaze toward the future. We look with eyes and hearts in expectant anticipation of Divine power and creative action. Living in the celebratory rhythm of the coming of Christ through Advent is a humbling and awesome ritual of the Christian faith.

The yearly family ritual has been such a touchstone of God's stability in love and grace within my life from the first years of my memory. Regardless of what else was going on in life when the season of Advent came, this liturgy centered my heart and drew my attention to prepare for the yearly coming of Jesus' new life within my life and inspired me to share it with my closest companions. It takes intentionality to sustain this prayer liturgy throughout the season and across the years, especially during the busyness and preparations for the coming of Christ during the Advent season. It is easy for this weekly family liturgy to get pushed aside. Christmas pageants, concerts, shopping, baking, church work, and Sunday evening youth group can all encroach upon the weekly Sunday evening gathering for this faith-forming family ritual.

My heart turns to wonder at this midpoint of your Advent journey. How is your journey going thus far? At this point on your journey through the Advent season, have you come upon bumps in the road? How are the terrain of your soul and the weekly practice of mandala creation inspiring your heart to new wisdom and joy? Has your schedule overwhelmed the practice of your pictorial journal? Is your spirit fully engaged in the rhythm of daily prayer and retreat while you read the devotionals? Could this book itself be an invitation to you to ignite for the first time this soul-deep love of listening for the Divine whisper? Could this retreat encourage you to pick up again the joy of lighting the wreath with your own family?

Your Companions This Week

As your inward journey continues this week, you are accompanied by Mary and her cousin Elizabeth, who model for us the joy of spiritual companionship. This week we often read the Gospel of Luke 1:39–56, which highlights the urgency and joy of Mary's visit to Elizabeth. This time of spiritual companioning provides opportunity for God's shared presence between them to shape their lives more deeply into the unique image of God for which they were created. This is the classic definition of the process of spiritual formation, when one is open to becoming more nearly formed by God into the image of Christ. This process of being shaped inwardly by God to become more Christ-like in attitude, actions, and behavior is not just for Mary and Elizabeth, but bears the fruit of Jesus' love for all humanity.

A unique gift of spiritual companionship is practicing an active listening technique called three-way listening. In this practice, a participant is listening to the other while at the same time both are listening for the powerful Divine whisper of God. Can you imagine the rich, spirit-filled conversation Mary and Elizabeth shared over their three-month visit while both listened to the other and God with the inner ear of the heart?

In the beginning of this Lukean text, Elizabeth hears simple words of greeting from Mary and instantly "the child leapt in her womb. And Elizabeth was filled with the Holy Spirit and exclaimed with a loud cry, 'Blessed are you among women, and blessed is the fruit of your womb'" (Luke 1:41–42). Elizabeth recognizes God's activity within her and cannot hold back from spontaneously offering a blessing of great joy. Practicing three-way listening in spiritual companionship deepens and expands awareness of God for all persons involved in the conversation and holds the potential for us to experience great joy in the discovery that God's presence is alive and well! For Mary, during this extended retreat at Elizabeth's house, she grows into her new identity as the chosen, beloved mother of God's son. During this faith-forming visit with a loved and trusted spiritual companion, the terrain of Mary's heart shifts, moving from surprise and consent to bearing God's son to spontaneous joy bursting forth in songs of praise.

The song of praise she offers is called the Magnificat (Luke 1:46–56), which expresses not only her own joy at the quickening of God's new life within her, but also a broader soul-deep knowing of the universal human and Divine dance of love. For me, this Divine dance of God's encircling love reconciling the world to God's self is symbolically depicted in the evergreen boughs of the Advent wreath. Through the candle-lighting liturgy emphasizing four simple virtues of Jesus— hope, love, joy, and peace—we are encircled by the heart of God and shaped by God's forgiveness and redemptive love. When community shares this liturgy together, we become spiritual companions on this faith-forming journey toward new birth.

Your Inward Journey

Just as with Mary and Elizabeth, your own journey of the heart continues this week as we ponder soul-deep joy and spiritual companionship. You may come with doubts, questions, and overextension of heart and mind in the harried season of Advent, but from these struggles comes the opportunity to open the way for God to make possible what may appear to be an impossible dream. Each of us has our own seemingly impossible dreams, maybe reconciliation with an estranged friend or family member, a new job, greater joy in the circumstances of life, or perhaps a new health diagnosis and the dream of healing. What is your dream that feels and looks nearly impossible to you? To turn an apparently impossible dream into reality by the grace of God, it is important to have trusted companions on the journey who stand in solidarity with you, looking toward new life.

This week, as you pause in reflection and prayer on your Advent spiritual *adventure*, consider who your spiritual companions are. When has your heart leapt with joy as the power of God reveals new possibility, and who did you share it with? Contemplate this leap of joy. This week as you focus on Mary's great joy of claiming fully her identity as the bearer of the Messiah, you may notice the quickening of Jesus' new life within your life, shifting the landscape of your heart as the *adventure* of this Advent expands your imagination. May God's mystery of unfathomable knowing encircle your heart as you experience the gifts of God this week.

THE THIRD SUNDAY OF ADVENT: A CREATIVE ARTS PRAYER PRACTICE

Audio Divina—*The Soul's Song*

Music! Music is something that every generation has been drawn to. From the earliest of times, rhythm has been tapped, drummed, hummed, listened to, and sung! There are a plethora of genres for music lovers to select their favorite sound, rhythm, and style. Toes go tapping, fingers snapping, hearts relaxing, and the soul starts to soar with the tunes as the music soaks into the mind and body.

Music is a companion for the soul. It can speak softly, whisper gently, and carry the soul upon the Divine wings of flight. My son is a musician. I love to watch him play his music. His entire body is engaged, even if only his fingers and arms are placed upon the instrument. It is as if his heart pours out through the notes and melodies as he plays. To me, it seems that he expresses his inward posture through the dissonance and harmonies of the music. As he plays, tensions seep away, joy is born, and wholeness in his being seems to come into focus.

The prayer practice this week is *audio divina*. The derivative of this word is from the Latin meaning "to hear, or to listen for, the Divine." As you listen for the Divine whisper through music, your heart will be set free to soar on Jesus' Christmas birthing in your life as hope gives way to new possibilities. The intention for this prayer experience is to let your soul sink deeply into the music so that, like my son, your soul may give expression beyond words to its outpouring of wisdom, emotion, and intuitive sense of the Christ rising with new insights and wisdom within you. As you will read, the practical technique for *audio divina* follows the format of *visio divina*, the prayer practice in week two.

The Challenges of *Audio Divina*

Music can be a powerful whisper of Divine formation, spiritual connection, and influence throughout our entire lives. However, if the music you listen to is too familiar, there may be no space for God's new wisdom and insight to be birthed in your heart, because your mind may associate the music with earlier experience. Or if the music is only an accompaniment to support the message of the lyrics, then your mind may be captured by the words and the music remains only background support.

To listen in a prayerful way, which opens space within your imagination for God's new wisdom and joy to speak directly to your heart, instrumental music that you have never heard before will be most inspiring. Ideally, music that carries soulfulness in its foundation will be most helpful. One such example of soulful music harkens back to the rich musical heritage of the North American continent—the soulful music of the Native American flute provides a serenade for the spirit.

Native American music expresses a deep spirituality that connects the listener to all of creation. The heartbeat rhythm of drumming takes our own heartbeats beyond the self and anchors them into that of community and all of creation. In this way the music becomes a spiritual companion uniting past and present with the cosmic future essence of God.

Grounded in an earthy spirituality, the Native American flute comes from the tender craft of expert hands hollowing out a branch and strategically placing finger holes so the breath from the flutist can create a soul-deep serenade. This soul-deep sound carries both the heartache and joy of the history of indigenous people of the United States. The sole drone and playful notes bring both the pain and suffering of the Trail of Tears and the joy of living in deep connection with the earth and God's creation.

The intent of today's creative arts experience is for you to simply notice the prayer that wells up within as you lovingly listen with the hope and anticipation of experiencing God's presence through *audio divina*.

Practicing *Audio Divina*

Plan at least thirty minutes for this prayer practice.

On this third Sunday of Advent, to prepare for listening to this musical reflection, please have your Bible open to Luke 1:39–56. You may choose to listen to any genre of music that captures your heart's attention, with the consideration of the parameters previously mentioned—ideally instrumental music you are unfamiliar with. For the enhanced option of soulful Native American music, Rev. Dr. Karen Covey Moore created a flute recording for this *audio divina* prayer practice. This musical reflection was born from her contemplation on the scripture of Mary's visitation to her cousin Elizabeth (Luke 1:39–56). Consider this quote from Rev. Moore about the movements of this music that inspired her as she played this reflection:

> The first part is where I am imagining Mary pondering the visit of the angel and asking, "Can it be?" and deciding to visit Elizabeth. The second part is her journey from Nazareth where she hurries to see if what the angel said is true and continues to ask, "Can it be?" The third part is Elizabeth's greeting, and the fourth part is the Magnificat.[1]

To access this recording, please enter the following link into your browser: http://goo.gl/WORgw1.

You may recall from week one the ancient practice of *lectio divina*. This same technique will be used as you read the scripture and listen to the music. You may alternate between reading the scripture and listening to the music during this time of *audio divina* if that is helpful to expand your imagination. Or read the text first, consider it prayerfully, and then begin *audio divina* with the musical selection of your choice. Please read the full instructions for *audio divina* before beginning your prayer experience.

1. *The first listening.* Music touches the human heart deeply. Consider: What emotions from this music rise within me and catch my attention?

2. *The second listening.* The most intimate of our experiences of God are also the most universal expressions of humanity. Consider: What sense of justice and journey arises within me as I listen to my musical selection and weave that together with the pilgrimage of Mary to Elizabeth? How does the music express release of struggle turned into soul-deep joy? How does the music encourage a sense of spiritual companionship as the drone and the melody harmonize together?

3. *The third listening.* Consider: What is the invitation to me whispered by God's prayer and presence through the weaving of this music and the scripture?

As you come into your sacred space, bringing your laptop if available or sitting at your desktop to listen to the music, offer a prayer anointing this space. Bring to your consciousness the possibility and expectation that in this space you will hear God's whispers to your heart as you listen. You may use this prayer or one of your own for anointing your sacred space:

Holy One, Holy Three, encircle me during this time. Let the music of your soul seep over me. May the melodies of your love penetrate the depths of my being and form within me an imaginative pilgrimage to your heart. As I journey with Mary through the barren land, with its valleys and hills, to joyously unite with Elizabeth, encourage me to dream. Unite my heart with the ancient rhythm of our Native American brothers and sisters through all the ages. As I listen, may I remember the Trail of Tears through the barrenness of American history and bring a peace-filled resolve to companions on this journey to new birthing. Open wide my imagination of Jesus, so that my eyes may see and my ears might hear the passion of your song for all your people. Help me to notice what my soul is captured by through this audio divina *practice. Grant me the courage to discover your invitation for my current living, as I am united through music with the ancestral way. I trust you, Lord, for the gifts and guidance on my creative awakening this day. Amen.*

To begin, sit comfortably, and focus your listening and heart upon the music. Take a few deep cleansing breaths as you sit quietly preparing to listen to your musical selection. Breathe in slowly, drawing the Spirit of God into your awareness. Fill your lungs with the creative possibility of God's vision. Slowly exhale all resistance and busyness from your day, leaving space for God to fill your heart and imagination. Release any indifference or resistance within you, allowing your heart to experience the allure of God's love drawing you into the music. Remember Blaise Pascal's image that all humans are created with a God-shaped emptiness within us that only God can fill, so releasing resistance and busyness assists in making the heart ready to receive God.

As you wait in this space, expanding the emptiness and openness within you before God, invite God to speak to you through your chosen instrumental music. Trust that God's Word is creatively present, ready to speak directly to your heart.

To assist in this *audio divina* prayer practice, I have provided a few thoughtful questions to stir your imagination and expand your awareness of God's presence:

- ☀ How does God invite you into this music?
- ☀ What is it about this music that draws your heart's attention?
- ☀ How do you imagine what you are most attracted to in this music could be God's voice whispering a wooing love song to your heart?
- ☀ What is God saying to you through this music?

⊕ What about this music inspires joy in your heart?

⊕ What could this music be telling you about spiritual companion-ship, which has encircled your heart over the years and is encir-cling your heart now as you seek God's presence and power?

Your Mandala: Listening Beyond Words for the Power of a Divine Whisper

The creation of your mandala is the daily retreat throughout this devo-tional book. It takes intentional time, focus, and prayer to allow God to silence all distractions of heart and create your mandala. From your *audio divina* prayer exercise, consider the landscape of your heart. How have the seasons of your spiritual life impacted your current thoughts and wordless wonders of your spirit? No need to try to articulate these insights of God's powerful whisper; simply creating marks and colors on the page can give them expression. I invite you to draw your empty mandala circle as a symbol of the God-shaped emptiness within your soul where you desire to experience Jesus' new Christmas birthing. As you fill the circle with colorful expression, you continue your spiritual journey toward Divine birthing during this Advent season. You will focus on the terrain of your heart all this third week as you notice the gifts of spiritual companionship and joyful presence of God.

Gather your tools of illumination: journal, pen, sketch pad, and colored pencils. Come into God's presence and settle yourself into your sacred space. After your time of *audio divina*, take your sketch pad and prayerfully draw your sacred circle for the creation of your mandala for today. As you gaze at the beauty of the empty space, ponder God's possibilities. Let the colors of your spirit wash over the circle of your mandala.

⊕ As you begin the creation of your mandala you may choose to consider:

✤ What color represents the feeling of your spirit after listen-ing to your reflective musical selection?

✤ How has this music inspired joy in your spirit?

✤ How did you notice the power of God's presence through your hearing?

❖ What sensations, thoughts, energies, emotions arise within you through this music?
❖ What colors best express these energies and emotions?
❖ As you let the Word of God write your reflections through the drawing of your mandala, consider abstract expression, concrete images, or a mixture of both in the creation of your mandala.

Pause here to create your mandala, expressing the felt sense of God's prayer and presence that you experienced during your contemplative listening of the musical selection of your choosing.

When you have completed your prayerful listening, offer a silent prayer of thanksgiving to God for new insights and wonders that have crossed your mind during this prayer and the experience of creating your mandala.

To Dream ...
the Impossible Dream

Luke 1:26–38

"Nothing is impossible with God."
Luke 1:37 NIV

To live the impossible dream ... to know with clarity of heart ... This is our quest of Advent: to hear beyond what seems physically possible, to know beyond what is logically proven, to reach beyond known experiences and extend our hearts to experience the Divine presence and receive the whisper of God's transforming Word. To believe what Mary first heard from the angel upon being chosen to be the mother of God's own love. To trust when our hearts are too weary and when our spirit is drooping. Our Advent *advent*ure is to follow the Way and to walk in the Light.

We have glanced within at "the dark night of the soul." We have encountered through our lifetimes dreams that have been broken, hopes that have been dashed, and yet our tenacious spirit reaches for the stars. New beginnings are born, new hope rises, as the truth of God's Word fills our interior knowing: nothing *is* impossible with God.

Advent is about virginal experiences—those times in life when you experience something that you have never done before. It is when what has seemed impossible comes into focus and is bursting forth into new possibility by the grace and presence of God.

From the first chapter of the Gospel of Luke, Mary asks the most obvious question when the angel Gabriel announces to her that she will become pregnant: "How can this be?" (Luke 1:34). How indeed! How can God create life out of seemingly lifeless situations? When we encounter virginal new things we, like Mary, ask, "How can this be?" How can

God bear the fruits of dreams that have been dashed and broken, remaking them and molding them into a living reality of resurrection? How can God give courage when we feel overwhelmed, afraid, or uncertain in life? What are your "How can this be?" questions? To experience a visible depiction of this kind of hidden miracle, visit the northern hemisphere during the wintry months and take a look outside at the seemingly brittle and lifeless trees. Yet hidden within the inward most part of the trees is the potential for new life. With the shifting of seasons and with spring's approach, what seems dead will spring to new life.

The angel answers Mary's most innocent and sincere question by proclaiming the power and the presence of the Divine whispering Word, which does indeed create new life and new possibility:

> The angel said to her, "Do not be afraid, Mary, for you have found favor with God. And now, you will conceive in your womb and bear a son, and you will name him Jesus. He will be great, and will be called the Son of the Most High, and the Lord God will give to him the throne of his ancestor David. He will reign over the house of Jacob for ever, and of his kingdom there will be no end." Mary said to the angel, "How can this be, since I am a virgin?" The angel said to her, "The Holy Spirit will come upon you, and the power of the Most High will overshadow you; therefore the child to be born will be holy; he will be called Son of God."
> Luke 1:30–35

And with this powerful whispered Word, resurrection is born into humanity. To prove the reality of God's powerful, life-creating Word, the angel tells of Elizabeth's miraculous conception in the barrenness of her old age:

> "And now, your relative Elizabeth in her old age has also conceived a son; and this is the sixth month for her who was said to be barren. For nothing will be impossible with God."
> Luke 1:36–37

Sometimes I wonder if humanity has lost hope in dreaming the impossible dream. Do broken dreams, entrapments of circumstance, weary egos, and misspoken words so mark the human experience that the power of God's Word is missed? Could God be MIA? I trust not! God is never missing in action. God the Creator of the universe and stars, God the Giver of Life in the hiddenness of the womb and heart *is* present in *all* of life, even in that which appears impossible.

Your Mandala: Listening Beyond Words for the Power of a Divine Whisper

Gather your tools of illumination: journal, pen, sketch pad, and colored pencils. Come into God's presence and settle yourself into your sacred space. Upon your sketch pad prayerfully draw your sacred circle for the creation of your mandala for today. As you gaze at the beauty of the empty space, ponder God's possibilities.

- ⊕ Pause. Center yourself by breathing deeply of God's infilling Spirit, letting go of all resistances and negativity within your heart.
- ⊕ Please read and ponder prayerfully Luke 1:26–38.
- ⊕ For an enhanced online option, place the words from Luke 1:26–38 beside the lyrics to the song "The Impossible Dream."[2] To access the words to "The Impossible Dream," please enter "The Impossible Dream lyrics" or the following link into your browser: https://goo.gl/CkDj2Z. (To hear the lyrics sung, use this link: http://goo.gl/hikYyJ.)
    - ✤ What images arise to your awareness as you read these two sets of words side by side?
- ⊕ Let the colors of your spirit flow into the mandala as you begin to draw, considering:
    - ✤ How is the inkling of Advent joy beginning to dawn within your spirit?
        - ❈ What new and virginal thing could God be beginning to birth into your living?
        - ❈ If nothing new has arisen for you yet, don't be concerned. God is still whispering; the advent of Jesus' birthing is still coming and is not yet upon us.
    - ✤ When have you experienced healing through broken dreams? What was that like for you?

❖ How was God present to, in, and through you as new life came into reality through the healing of broken dreams and the disappointments in life turned into possibility?

❖ How has God anointed your healing so that as you heal you are able to assist, care for, and companion others on their journey through difficult times of life?

⊕ As you let the Word of God write your reflections in the drawing of your mandala, ponder the hope of Advent's dawning.

❖ What colors are you drawn to?

❖ Consider abstract expression, concrete images, or a mixture of both in the creation of your mandala.

❖ At this stage on your Advent journey, who are your spiritual companions, and who have you companioned?

❖ What colors reflect your experience of spiritual companionship?

❖ How has the landscape of your inward being shifted during this daily retreat and Advent devotional reading time?

I encourage you to strive to create a mandala for each daily reflection. This pictorial journey of reflection beyond words will awaken new possibility through God's wooing whispers as you listen for the advent of God's call this holy season.

Sit back and receive the anointing as the dawning of God's new birth becomes reality in your life. Enjoy the creative expression of God. If creating a mandala for today fails to inspire your heart, consider writing a journal entry, poem, or prayer to express God's soul-deep joy dancing in union with your spirit.

Upon completion of your mandala, offer a silent prayer of gratitude in humility for the persistent presence of God in the midst of humanity, for with God, nothing is impossible. Celebrate the companions that have walked with you through these times of life and honor the soul-deep joy of God within you.

Sojourners and Companions

Luke 1:39–45

If we are to dream, *if* we are to trust beyond logic and reasoning, *if* we consent to the virginal new birthing of God's Word into our life, *then* surely we will need companions to walk beside us through the hidden interior shifting of the heart's terrain as the labor pains birth new reality into being.

Human beings are created for community. It may be a small community of two or as large as hundreds. It is not the size of community that matters but rather the shared presence. Shared presence is an acknowledgment of the connection of the Christ in you and the Christ in me. We don't always articulate it this way. Mostly we name shared presence, the connection between folks, as just being friendly.

No matter the depth of intimacy and love for God, from the beginning God created folks for community. Adam longed for Eve. Jesus sent the disciples on the itinerant way of ministry in twos. Remember Saint Francis, the humble leader who inspired people to find God in all things, and his most devoted follower, Saint Clare? Their deep, abiding friendship was shared through conversation, prayer, and spending time in one another's company. They enjoyed sharing silence that was rich with the fullness of God's presence. It is through the body, the corporal house of the spirit, that incarnation is born and experienced. Together we become companions sharing the journey toward deeper intimacy in God. Together insights and prayers are shared as companions respond to John Wesley's question of spiritual accountability: "How is it with your soul?"[3]

Even before the first "quickening of life" within her, before the first flutter of the presence of God creating life, Mary recognized her need and desire for spiritual companionship:

At that time Mary got ready and hurried to a town in the hill country.
Luke 1:39 NIV

This little phrase provides emphasis of how intentional each pilgrim must be on the journey of faith. Pilgrims on the verge of birthing new life, as the old self-image, mannerisms, or attitudes shift, are to prepare for this new posture of heart by making spiritual companions a priority for discernment on the journey. Spiritual companions assist with the pilgrim's telling of his or her own story, listening for the hills and valleys of desire and resistance on the sojourn toward the heart of God. It takes intentionality to show up and listen for the hidden dance of God's song whispering to the heart. And the humble, deliberate act of receiving happens as one seeks companions on this pilgrim way. The act of giving and receiving blessing is never haphazard. It always shows intention.

I thumbed through a little picture book several years ago. Sorry, I don't know the title or author, but the parable stuck with me. This book featured a dog who desperately wants to give his dear friend, another dog, a very special gift. The Gifter had often heard his human companions mention something called *nothing*. It seemed to the Gifter a very common item:

> "There is *nothing* to eat!"
> "There is *nothing* on television, even with hundreds of stations!"
> "I went to the store and found *nothing* to buy."

Surely the gift of *nothing* must be special, since folks always talked about it, thought the Gifter. So the little doggy Gifter trotted to the store to find *nothing*, but he found *lots* of things. He sat and stared at the television, but there was *a lot* on the screen to watch! And when the Gifter stood in front of the refrigerator, *lots* and *lots* of food was stacked in there. The Gifter was stumped in trying to find the perfect gift of *nothing*. Finally the Gifter decided on an empty box. He wrapped it up and gave it to his doggy friend. The other dog was very excited to receive the gift. With great anticipation he carefully unwrapped the precious present and exclaimed, "There is *nothing* in here!" "Exactly!" said the Gifter. Joy filled the two friends as they spent the rest of the day sitting together, enjoying one another's companionship.

It takes intentionality to share presence with another. Shared presence is the gift of God's invisible, connective, wooing love song from one soul to another.

> When Elizabeth heard Mary's greeting, the child leapt in her womb. And Elizabeth was filled with the Holy Spirit.
> Luke 1:41

Intentionality between spiritual companions causes even the most simple of words to be filled with the holy presence of Divine light and power. And in an instant, with the whisper of the Word, blessing is given as blessing is received, and the two become as one in the heart of God on the pilgrimage to new birth.

> And Elizabeth was filled with the Holy Spirit and exclaimed with a loud cry, "Blessed are you among women, and blessed is the fruit of your womb. And why has this happened to me, that the mother of my Lord comes to me? For as soon as I heard the sound of your greeting, the child in my womb leapt for joy. And blessed is she who believed that there would be a fulfillment of what was spoken to her by the Lord."
> Luke 1:41–45

 Your Mandala: Listening Beyond Words for the Power of a Divine Whisper

Gather your tools of illumination: journal, pen, sketch pad, and colored pencils. Come into God's presence and settle yourself into your sacred space. Upon your sketch pad prayerfully draw your sacred circle for the creation of your mandala for today. As you gaze at the beauty of the empty space, ponder God's possibilities.

- ⊕ Pause. Center yourself by breathing deeply of God's infilling Spirit, letting go of all resistances and negativity within your heart.
- ⊕ Please read and ponder prayerfully Luke 1:39–45.
- ⊕ Consider the parable of the little dog.

⊕ Let the colors of your spirit flow into the mandala as you begin to draw, considering:

   ❖ Who are your companions—those on this Advent pilgrimage around the world and in your community, possibly reading this book at the same time as you? Your companions are folks who sojourn with you through life. These could be friends, prayer partners, your spiritual director, a family member—whoever walks with you through life.

      ✷ How is the presence of Christ experienced and known in this companionship of community?

      ✷ Who are your companions in the Spirit?

      ✷ What difference does sharing God's presence with another make in your life?

   ❖ How do you gain clarity of heart and discernment on the journey of your faith pilgrimage? Does anyone accompany you on this journey? Possibly a spiritual director could listen and assist you on the discerning way to new life.

⊕ Instead of contemplating any question, you may simply desire to create a spiritual companionship mandala. What does companionship feel like, look like, within your heart? How does God connect you with others? Give expression to the great joy of this companionship through your wordless wonders as you draw your mandala.

⊕ As you let the Word of God write your reflections in the drawing of your mandala, ponder the hope of Advent's dawning.

   ❖ What colors are you drawn to?

   ❖ Consider abstract expression, concrete images, or a mixture of both in the creation of your mandala.

   ❖ How does the choice of colors reflect your choices on the spiritual path at this stage of your Advent *adventure*?

I encourage you to strive to create a mandala for each daily reflection. This pictorial journey of reflection beyond words will awaken new possibility through God's wooing whispers as you listen for the advent of God's call this holy season.

Sit back and receive the anointing as the dawning of God's new birth becomes reality in your life. Enjoy the creative expression of God. If creating a mandala for today fails to inspire your heart, consider writing a journal entry, poem, or prayer to express your holy experience of spiritual companionship and soul-deep joy.

Upon completion of your mandala, offer a silent prayer of gratitude for companions who walk beside you on your spiritual pilgrimage.

Inward Groaning

Romans 8:22–28
Psalm 5:1–3

New things, situations, or people almost always cause us to pause. Inward thoughts, doubts, second guesses can easily plague the mind when newness of life is encountered. A few wonders that may arise as God dawns new things in the midst of our usual routine:

- Am I doing the right thing?
- Is this what God really wants from me or for me?
- Whom do I need to collaborate with me to accomplish this new thing?
- How do I notice God's calling as God whispers invitation to me for this new thing?
- What is the goal of this new thing?
- Who will be affected?
- What effect will the new opportunity, experience, feeling, event have on my life?
- Will my understanding of God shift as newness ripples through my life and soul? If so, how?
- What will I do to nurture, sustain, and expand this new happening in my life?
- How will I celebrate what God has done and is doing?

The inward groaning of new life echoes in the heart of God as humans struggle with stretching attitudes, self-image, reactions, and responses to God's new things. Mary knew inward groaning as life formed within her and her life was forever changed (Luke 1). Being pregnant by the holy presence of God may have shifted her understanding of how God intervenes and acts in the realm of humanity. Or maybe she always knew of God's activity in her life, but this was simply the first time she experienced God's intervention in her life through pregnancy. As a young woman engaged to marry, she may have dreamed of someday becoming a mother, but *now* the young Mary faces the reality of new life within her. The inward groans within Mary's heart may have been fear—wondering how to break the news to her parents, to Joseph, and to her Nazarene neighbors. Or the sigh of her heart could possibly have been that of amazement, excitement, longing, and humility, with newly deepened faith formation.

Inward groaning accompanies spiritual awakening as you consent to the whispers of God's call breaking into your life. Sometimes, as in Mary's case, even the corporeal body grows and stretches with the new life that God is creating within us. The new life of God breaks into everyday living and transforms us from the inside to our outside actions. There *is* a groaning, a shift of interior formation as God's Word opens new thoughts, new feelings, new hopes and dreams, or whispers comfort, peace, and healing mercies. Along with this interior formation, the groans of outward actions and disciplines stretch habitual ways of former thinking and doing. New actions, expressions of attitude, and works of justice are born from the inward groaning of the soul. Within Romans 8:22–28 we hear:

> We know that the *whole creation has been groaning* as in the pains of childbirth right up to the present time. Not only so, but we ourselves, who have the firstfruits of the Spirit, groan inwardly as we wait eagerly for our adoption to sonship, the redemption of our bodies. For in this hope we were saved. But hope that is seen is no hope at all. Who hopes for what they already have? But if we hope for what we do not yet have, we wait for it patiently.
>
> In the same way, the Spirit helps us in our weakness. We do not know what we ought to pray for, but the Spirit himself intercedes for us through *wordless groans.* And he who searches our hearts knows the mind of the Spirit, because the *Spirit intercedes* for God's people in accordance with the will of God.
>
> And we know that in all things God works for the good of those who love him, who have been called according to his purpose.
>
> Romans 8:22–28 NIV (emphasis added)

Groaning comes as we wait. Soul-deep sighing comes as we seek. The Spirit cries out as we intentionally strive for the fullness of God to birth our most authentic life. Today we pause to reflect upon our inward groaning. Is it a groan of hope? Could the groaning of resistance be sounding within your inner heart? Maybe the groaning of heart within is not something that you are even consciously aware of, yet there is a yearning or an emptiness that occasionally pokes into your consciousness. If you are not consciously aware of inward groaning and growth toward the heart of God, then spend time this day asking God for discerning wisdom as you listen with the inner ear of your heart.

A possible prayer that may assist in discerning God's wisdom and the inward groaning of your heart is: "Jesus, help me to notice your inward desire, your groans of spirit within me, so that I may become more aware of your ever-deepening love shaping my interior heart." This is a prayer that has the possibility to open further the spiral of formation as you descend nearer the vortex of God's energetic, tornadic whirlwind of interior formation through this Advent season. Through this time of prayer, may God gift you with a sense of God's presence and a hearing of your inward groaning of spirit stretching you to new possibilities.

The shifting of the terrain of the heart can be scary as you recognize God's little nudges calling you into new experiences. New experiences include but are certainly not limited to increased courage, peace, hope, joy, stamina for daily relationships, and authentic boldness in lightly held love. I encourage you not to let the darkness of fear snuff out the glowing ember of new possibility. As you pray with the Romans text this day, let the assurance of God's word from Jeremiah anchor your reflection: "For surely I know the plans I have for you, says the Lord, plans for your welfare and not for harm, to give you a future with hope" (Jeremiah 29:11).

There is no need for fear. God desires good for you!

🌀 *Your Mandala: Listening Beyond Words for the Power of a Divine Whisper*

Gather your tools of illumination: journal, pen, sketch pad, and colored pencils. Come into God's presence and settle yourself into your sacred space. Upon your sketch pad prayerfully draw your sacred circle for the creation of your mandala for today. As you gaze at the beauty of the empty space, ponder God's possibilities.

⊕ Pause. Center yourself by breathing deeply of God's infilling Spirit, letting go of all resistances and negativity within your heart.

⊕ Let the colors of your spirit flow into the mandala, as you create a mandala from prayerful listening for and to the inward groaning of your spirit. How is God inviting you to something new?

⊕ To assist with your deep listening, you may want to sit with Psalm 5:1–3. I have provided two translations for your prayer time:

Listen, GOD! Please, 　pay attention! Can you make sense of these 　ramblings, my groans and cries? King-God, I need your help. Every morning you'll hear me at it again. Every morning I lay out the pieces of my life on your altar and watch for fire to descend.	Give ear to my words, 　O LORD; consider my groaning. Give attention to the sound 　of my cry, my King and my God, for to you do I pray. O LORD, in the morning you 　hear my voice; in the morning I prepare 　a sacrifice for you and 　watch.
From *The Message*	From the English Standard Version

⊕ What inward groaning do you sense this day?

⊕ As you let the Word of God write your reflections in the drawing of your mandala, ponder the hope of Advent's dawning.

✤ What colors are you drawn to?

✤ Consider abstract expression, concrete images, or a mixture of both in the creation of your mandala.

✤ How does the choice of colors reflect your choices on the spiritual path at this stage of your Advent *advent*ure?

I encourage you to strive to create a mandala for each daily reflection. This pictorial journey of reflection beyond words will awaken new possibility through God's wooing whispers as you listen for the advent of God's call this holy season.

Sit back and receive the anointing as the dawning of God's new birth becomes reality in your life. Enjoy the creative expression of God. If creating a mandala for today fails to inspire your heart, consider writing a journal entry, poem, or prayer to express God's sighs, which may seem too deep for words and yet fill your senses with soul-deep joy.

Upon completion of your mandala, offer a silent prayer of gratitude for this time of deep listening and crying out with groans of your spirit to God as you continue your Advent *adven*ture into the holiness of Jesus' new birth.

From Humble Beginnings

Isaiah 11:1–9

I was hungry! I went to bed hungry the other night. It was an intentional act. I did have food in the kitchen. *It was tempting me.* My stomach growled and churned. It was a pesky feeling to have something gnawing from the inside of my being, calling me to awareness when my entire being just wanted to rest, relax, and sleep. Before sleep could come to me, by my intention, I engaged my heart and soul in an act. I went to bed hungry because I truly wanted to pray in solidarity with the children around this world who go to bed almost every night with stomachs groaning and insides churning, with pangs of hunger their only bedtime rhythm and lullaby.

I was reminded again that night that all I am in ministry and all that I do is not just for me, for the edification and resting of my soul in God's amazing grace and for receiving God's wooing whispers of love. My heart yearns for this special time of lounging with God, and I enjoy every moment of resting there. Yet even going on retreat, either away geographically from normal routines and duties or retreating with unseen companions through the mysterious connection of Christ with the assistance of the printed word or Internet, I know in the depths of my soul it is not just for me.

Remember from the very first day of this retreat, in the introduction to icon gazing, we learned to look beyond the surface? We are called to listen to the interior movement of God beyond the surface level of facts and events of life. It is in the hidden heart of life that the spiral of formation draws us ever closer to the heart of God, in whose image we have been created. Yet the amazing thing about this descending spiral of God's formation is this: the closer we come to the vortex, the closer we come to the heart of God, the closer we also become to humanity. I went to bed hungry not for me but for the sake of hungry children around the world. Through the prophet Isaiah we are called to become more than self-seekers of God's new thing in the birth of Jesus.

Please pause and read Isaiah 11:1–9. In the text we read:

> A shoot shall come out from the stump of Jesse,
> and a branch shall grow out of his roots.
> > Isaiah 11:1

A root from the stump of Jesse—what an image! From that which looks dead and lifeless comes forth the birthing of new life and spiritual lineage. A new covenant with God's people was an intentional act. I wonder if God had intentional sleepless nights to ponder and pray, to be in solidarity with humanity who is steeped in hungers and spiritual malnutrition, physical poverty and brokenness, before deciding to come to earth in the human life of Jesus. From generation to generation, poverty and injustice, broken humanity and suffering have been present. In fact, Jesus said, "For you always have the poor with you, and you can show kindness to them whenever you wish; but you will not always have me" (Mark 14:7). Never in all the whispers of God's wooing Gospel of Good News does it state, "Well, folks, that is just the way it is. Let's pack it in and give up!"

From this all but dead stump of spiritual lineage comes a new branch. From humble beginnings comes resurrection hope: Jesus, this One through whom the power, presence, and energy of God will live and burst into accessibility for all of humanity. Because of this birthing season, the gift of resurrection and the presence of the Holy Spirit empowers us to live as agents of the here, the now, and the not yet, and into the still-to-come Peaceable Kingdom of God.

> The spirit of the Lord shall rest on him,
> the spirit of wisdom and understanding,
> the spirit of counsel and might,
> the spirit of knowledge and the fear of the Lord.
> His delight shall be in the fear of the Lord.
> > Isaiah 11:2–3

This birthing from the stump of tired and weary systematic faith brings about a new way of living for the sake of others. God's Peaceable

Kingdom coming upon earth will affect every living thing through all generations.

> He shall not judge by what his eyes see,
> or decide by what his ears hear;
> but with righteousness he shall judge the poor,
> and decide with equity for the meek of the earth;
> he shall strike the earth with the rod of his mouth,
> and with the breath of his lips he shall kill the wicked.
> Righteousness shall be the belt around his waist,
> and faithfulness the belt around his loins.
>
> Isaiah 11:3–5

The smallest of intentional acts from humanity will create a Kingdom of difference. No longer will gossip lead vision or relationship; manipulations to get others to do things "your way" will cease. Folks will learn the mystery of seeing beyond the surface and hearing beyond the spoken word. The presence of God will be transparent through actions and conversations. With the birth of Jesus, the ripples of resurrection from manger to the empty tomb anoint humanity to live as God's covenant people ever growing into the likeness of the Word that became flesh.

> The wolf shall live with the lamb,
> the leopard shall lie down with the kid,
> the calf and the lion and the fatling together,
> and a little child shall lead them.
> The cow and the bear shall graze,
> their young shall lie down together;
> and the lion shall eat straw like the ox.
> The nursing child shall play over the hole of the asp,
> and the weaned child shall put its hand on the adder's den.
> They will not hurt or destroy
> on all my holy mountain;
> for the earth will be full of the knowledge of the Lord
> as the waters cover the sea.
>
> Isaiah 11:6–9

Do you feel the excitement? Does the anticipation mount to soaring heights within your heart? The new Kingdom is dawning within. New possibility is about to be born. And we can make choices to aid in the birthing of God's presence on earth through our actions, our words, our prayers, and our desires as we stand in solidarity with others.

Your Mandala: Listening Beyond Words for the Power of a Divine Whisper

Gather your tools of illumination: journal, pen, sketch pad, and colored pencils. Come into God's presence and settle yourself into your sacred space. Upon your sketch pad prayerfully draw your sacred circle for the creation of your mandala for today. As you gaze at the beauty of the empty space, ponder God's possibilities.

- ⊕ Pause. Center yourself by breathing deeply of God's infilling Spirit, letting go of all resistances and negativity within your heart.
- ⊕ Spend significant time praying with the prophet Isaiah in Isaiah 11:1–9.
- ⊕ Let the colors of your spirit flow into the mandala as you begin to draw, considering:
  - ✤ As Jesus' Kingdom comes on earth as in heaven, how is God forming you to be a part of this dawning birth? Are you being invited to new action in the way that you companion others within your community?
  - ✤ Could the marking of your commitment to live into the Peaceable Kingdom be the call of your mandala for this day? Who will you stand in solidarity with as companion and friend in faith, bringing justice and mercy into this world?
- ⊕ As you let the Word of God write your reflections in the drawing of your mandala, ponder the hope of Advent's dawning.
  - ✤ What colors are you drawn to?
  - ✤ Consider abstract expression, concrete images, or a mixture of both in the creation of your mandala.
  - ✤ How does the choice of colors reflect your choices on the spiritual path at this stage of your Advent *adventure*?

I encourage you to strive to create a mandala for each daily reflection. This pictorial journey of reflection beyond words will awaken new possibility through God's wooing whispers as you listen for the advent of God's call this holy season.

Sit back and receive the anointing as the dawning of God's new birth becomes reality in your life. Enjoy the creative expression of God. If creating a mandala for today fails to inspire your heart, consider writing a journal entry, poem, or prayer to express the humble beginnings of God's new possibility rising from the stump of former things in your life.

Upon completion of your mandala, offer a silent prayer of gratitude for this time of deep listening. Mark your commitment to live as companions with others on the faith journey called life, as we strive to be in solidarity with others and lean into the joy of the Peaceable Kingdom.

My Magnificat

Luke 1:46–56

Oh the *joy* of consenting and saying *yes* to God! The energy and delight simply cannot be contained. Mary has a soul-deep knowing that led to her expression of praise and great joy. The energy and joy of God's presence secretly knitting together new life in her innermost being could not be contained. Her joy could not be restrained and her spirit could not be shut off from expression.

Why is it that as human beings we so often restrain ourselves when it comes to trusting that something miraculous of God is on the verge of birthing? At times we even talk ourselves out of believing that this amazing newness of God could happen to us personally. Or we don't want to appear to be religious fanatics, so we don't tell what we have learned from God's prophetic and living Word. Instead, we take a "wait and see" attitude, reasoning, "I will wait and see if this really happens before getting excited or saying anything." The inward groans of inadequacy, unworthiness, the "what ifs" and "if onlys" rear their heads and invade the human spirit, holding us captive while we forgo the proclamation of delight for God's activity in our lives. I wonder if folks overwhelmed with the busy lifestyle of the twenty-first century have become wall-flowers at the dance of God's joyous new birthing in our lives.

Today is about letting go. I make a distinction between "letting go" and "release." I have done work with folks in addiction and mental health ministry. The saying I hear often in this ministry is "Let go and let God." However, what I witness over and over again with folks who have great intentions to "let go and let God" is that almost as soon as this commitment is professed, the individual lets it go to God and then snatches it right back from God. The experience of giving to God and then snatching it back is not limited to those with addictive struggles and mental illness.

Humanity has become very skilled at snatching back what we thought has been turned over to God. Have you ever had this experience? You become attached to a certain desired outcome in a stressful situation, saying, "Thy will be done, but what I really desire is ..." Or during a time when worry and anxiety regarding a loved one are plaguing you, you let it go and then resume worrying. You may pray for God to remove this anxiety, offering it in prayer ... and yet in the wee hours of the night the same worry, the same anxiety, comes back into your thoughts and keeps sleep from coming. "Letting go and letting God" can be very difficult work.

As I consider our companion for this week, I wonder if Elizabeth through the years of barrenness ever let go of her monthly disappointment. Had she reached a point in her life and longing for a child that she accepted the improbability of becoming pregnant and resigned herself to a life without children? Was she able to "let go and let God," or did she ever snatch back her desire and continue petitioning God far beyond her childbearing years?

I don't think it is just semantics. For me there is a difference in our posture toward God between "letting go and letting God" and complete release. The image of release for me comes from a television commercial for Dawn dish detergent.[4] The commercial was created after the tragic oil rig explosion in the Gulf, when the oil spill stretched for hundreds of miles along beautiful coastal shores. This expansive oil slick wreaked destruction on the native wildlife. In the commercial, some ducklings, which are covered in oil, are being gently cleansed with Dawn. And with the magic of television, almost instantly these little ducklings stretch their cleansed wings, shake their feathers, and are released by the human hands that have held them so tenderly during the cleaning process. Swiftly the ducklings rise to flight. There is no sense of obligation from the ducklings to return to the humans, who have degreased their feathery down and released them into soaring freedom of flight. This full and complete release is unconditional and without expectation from both the duck and the human perspective. The animal lover is overjoyed to see them go and fully expect the released ducklings will *not* return. Wouldn't it be great if the interior groaning of heart could be released with full expectation to *not* return?

Today is about releasing. It is not just about letting go in the typical sense but about giving full and complete release to God. It is in releasing the thoughts, feelings, and inward groaning that imprison the soul that the soul is set free for individual and community alike. You may not even be consciously aware of what restrains your spirit and could be cutting off your freedom to join Mary in an explosion of song and dance for the new life God is forming within you this season. When you are ready, this flight of freedom for your soul can be expressed by joining Mary as she sings her poetic Magnificat, "My soul magnifies the Lord" (Luke 1:46). This new possibility of God is unique to each individual. God knows best what each of us needs to be drawn closer to God's heart.

Mary's Magnificat is beauty soaring on the wings of God's Word in flight as she fully consents to the formation of new life within the depth of her being. In that moment she becomes her most authentic self as originally created in the image of God to be the bearer of this new God life. With her intentional and complete consent to God's plan, releasing her self-made plans for her future, Mary's truest self emerges as she faithfully becomes the bearer of God. Her praise is unstoppable. Today I ask you to turn inward to consider how your soul is bursting with unstoppable praise as you join Mary in complete release of all that holds you back from the fullness of God's healing love and mercy in your life. Today you will write your own Magnificat.

ᚲᚱᚲ *Your Mandala: Listening Beyond Words for the Power of a Divine Whisper*

Gather your tools of illumination: journal, pen, sketch pad, and colored pencils. Come into God's presence and settle yourself into your sacred space. Upon your sketch pad prayerfully draw your sacred circle for the creation of your mandala for today. As you gaze at the beauty of the empty space, ponder God's possibilities.

⊕ Pause. Center yourself by breathing deeply of God's infilling Spirit, letting go of all resistances and negativity within your heart.

⊕ Please pray and read Luke 1:46–56.

⊕ Let the colors of your spirit flow into the mandala as you express the song of your heart in honor, reverence, and praise of God. Consider:

    ✤ Who are your companions on this holy way to authentic love and life?

    ✤ How does their presence give you courage to step into the unknown of God's preferred future?

    ✤ What are you surrendering to God in complete release this day, so that God's new possibilities in life may come into reality?

⊕ As you let the Word of God write your reflections in the drawing of your mandala, ponder the hope of Advent's dawning.

    ✤ What colors are you drawn to?

    ✤ Consider abstract expression, concrete images, or a mixture of both in the creation of your mandala.

    ✤ How does the choice of colors reflect your choices on the spiritual path as you pause on your Advent trek into new possibility and full release of former ways of thinking and being?

I encourage you to strive to create a mandala for each daily reflection. This pictorial journey of reflection beyond words will awaken new possibility through God's wooing whispers as you listen for the advent of God's call this holy season.

Sit back and receive the anointing as the dawning of God's new birth becomes reality in your life. Enjoy the creative expression of God. If creating a mandala for today fails to inspire your heart, consider writing a journal entry, poem, or prayer to revel in your soul-deep joy and offer praises to God for the marvelous things God is creating in you.

Upon completion of your mandala, offer a silent prayer of gratitude for this time of deep union with God's desire forming new birth and opportunity within you.

Saturday Sabbath

This week has been filled with *advent*ure and the folks who journey with us through this life. It is such a blessing to have soul friends who companion us on the ever-deepening way to authentic self, closer to the heart of God and closer to other folks. One of the attributes of this spiritual companionship is three-way listening. This gift of sacred story-telling and holy listening is the foundation of spiritual companioning as both parties listen for the interior movement of God. Today is your day to rest. Not just the body, but the spirit also needs to rest in quiet before God, without the need to seek deeper insights and wisdom. Truly, as we have read, "in God alone is my soul at rest" (Psalm 62:1).[5]

Now is the time to rest in the heart of God. What whispers have you heard from God this week? Would creating a mandala that expresses thanksgiving and awesome wonder at God's new possibilities within your life give your body and spirit the restful energy of this Sabbath day? Could laying your paper and colored pencils down and doing something totally different provide rejuvenation to your spirit? Maybe noticing all of the ingredients that go into baking your favorite cookies, leisurely stirring the batter, and forming circular cookie creations from the most elemental of ingredients will spark peaceful joy in your soul for today. If this option doesn't entice your spirit, you may desire to explore on your own one more *audio divina* prayer experience in order to listen for the song of your soul.

To practice *audio divina*, you can use any musical selection that is attractive to your soul. The genre of music is limited only by your interest. Prayerfully consider what musical selection you would like to use for prayer. A plethora of original music can be found on the Internet, or you may have a favorite instrumental piece that your heart is drawn to. It is recommended to practice *audio divina* with instrumental music rather than songs with lyrics. The soul is better equipped to hear the whisper of God's Word beyond the surface when music is void of lyrics.

❧ *Practicing* Audio Divina

Plan at least thirty minutes for this prayer practice. Pause now in prayer to begin *audio divina* for a musical reflection.

To begin, sit comfortably, and focus your eyes and heart upon the instrumental music. Let all busyness from the week fall away as you center yourself in God's presence. Allow the breath of God to fill you with restored peace and quiet this Sabbath day. Breathe in slowly, drawing the Spirit of God into your awareness, filling your lungs with the creative possibility of God's vision. Slowly exhale all resistance and busyness from your day, leaving space for God to fill your heart and imagination.

As you wait in this space, expanding the emptiness and openness within you before God, invite God to speak to you through this music. Trust that God's Word is creatively alive even through music to speak directly to your heart for your soul's edification.

To assist in this *audio divina* prayer practice, I have provided a few thoughtful questions to stir your imagination and expand your awareness of God's presence:

1. *The first listening.* Music touches the human heart deeply. Consider: What emotions from this music rose up within you and caught your attention?

2. *The second listening.* The most intimate of our experiences of God are also the most universal expressions of humanity. For example, if you experience God as comforter, your compassion can be expanded, knowing that God has compassion upon others, not just you. Consider: Where does this musical selection intersect with your life? How does it embrace your heart, and what thoughts are pricked within your mind when you listen to this musical piece?

3. *The third listening.* Consider: What is the invitation whispered to you by God's prayer and presence through the weaving of this

music and pondering the good news of Jesus' impending birth within your life?

However you choose to spend your Sabbath, you may offer this prayer or one of your own design as a conclusion to this holy Sabbath day:

> *Holy amazing God, One in Three and Three in One! My soul is captivated by your whispered Word sung to my heart. Anchor my soul through the music of your spirit that I may truly live as you love. Lead me into your desired new possibilities that are on the edge of creation within my life. Let my heart burst into glorious song and dance as I follow your lead within my life. I trust you and yearn to live as your beloved one. Amen.*

Rest well, my dear companions; rest nestled near the heart of God.

CELEBRATE! THE POWER OF A WHISPERED LIFE

New Life Springs Forth

*The time is coming. Hurry! Bring your hopes, bring
your dreams, bring your hurts, bring your pains, and
seek God's new birthing in the midst of life.*

Christmas is coming! The advent of God is preparing—silently, powerfully, hopefully desiring to break into the interior landscape of your
heart. Whether you have been in faith and love with Jesus for many
years or just coming to wonder who Jesus is and how Jesus loves and
lives within this world, the onset of God's new powerful presence is
imminent. Are you ready? Has your spirit grown calm in open receptivity over these past few weeks? I use the liturgical seasons of the Christian year—Advent, Lent (the forty days of preparation for Easter),
and holy week (the week immediately preceding Easter) as times of
yearly spiritual assessment. For me, these seasons are opportunities to
consider the terrain of my heart and the pliability of my spirit in God's
hands. This annual examen of spirit is an opportunity to notice how I
have grown, how I am being challenged, and where resistance to going
deeper into the heart of God is within me. When the first Advent candle is lit, my heart wonders how I daily, weekly, and through each cycle
of my life hope for and anticipate God's presence dawning in the midst
of my ordinary life. The second candle brings the wonder of love into
my heart—exactly how have I made loving God, self, and neighbor a
priority in my actions and relationships with others this year? How have
I experienced the stability of my faith as I was embraced with God's
love through both difficult and joyous times, increasing my love of God?
With the third candle, I reflect on the soul-deep joy I have experienced
throughout the year and the people I have shared it with. How would
you assess your spiritual *advent*ure through this Advent season thus far?

On the fourth Sunday of Advent, all four candles on the circumference of the wreath are lit. The final purple candle is traditionally known

to represent Jesus' virtue of peace. He is the one ushering in the Peaceable Kingdom through his birth, life, death, and resurrection. However, this Peaceable Kingdom, first envisioned by Isaiah—"The wolf will live with the lamb, the leopard will lie down with the goat, the calf and the lion and the yearling together; and a little child will lead them" (Isaiah 11:6)—is not yet complete. God is still forming each of us into God's great possibilities to live as Jesus loves on earth. When this Kingdom comes to completion, there will be no injustice, no suffering, and no destruction, and peace will come upon earth as in heaven.

As the fourth Advent candle is lit, we are invited to pray for wisdom in discerning how to embody this kind of peace throughout our lives. With the lighting of this candle, I wonder how I have intentionally lived peace in my personal relationships, in interpersonal relationships in my neighborhoods, and throughout the world. It is this candle that takes me back to the earliest days of the Christian church, before the division of denominations, prior to legislative rules of who is in and who is out. It harkens back to a time when early monastic Christians literally left the allure of the big cities such as Rome and Alexandria and sought an intentional lifestyle of simplicity and prayer in love of God. The early monastic Christians who left family, financial security, and social status to follow the descending way of Jesus' humility toward the Peaceable Kingdom of God found stability of faith through an austere life of constant prayer. The descending way of Jesus—remember from week two the image of the tornado depicting the descending spiral of faith formation as one matures and deepens in intimacy with God. For me, lighting this fourth candle is a symbol of the intentional desire to journey toward the celebration of the birth of Jesus with an ever-opening heart. An open heart releases ego-driven desires and opens inward space for the power and presence of God's peace to come anew to our life, through relationships both interpersonal and within community. Here in the anticipation of Jesus' birthing, transformation of heart and soul is noticed for those who follow his ways and seek to live peace on earth.

This leads us to the heart of Christmas on Christmas Eve, when the Christ candle is lit. With the lighting of the Christ candle, the believer claims again the reality that the light of Christ is breathed into humanity through Jesus' resurrected Holy Spirit of God. It is the Holy Spirit that illumines the darkness of the world and our individual lives with great new possibility.

Your Companions This Week

As you continue your inward journey of the heart this week, you are accompanied by a cast of characters and have the added expertise of wisdom writings from early Christian seekers, the monastic mothers and fathers of the desert. Chapter 2 of the Gospel of Luke is typically read during this week, both in regularly scheduled weekend worship celebrations and on Christmas Eve. Instantly upon reading this chapter the heart is drawn to Mary, her courageous "yes" as God's whisper of pregnancy put into motion the Divine plan of God's love birthing among all generations. Alongside Mary, the shepherds will guide us into exuberance of joy and peaceful empowerment, witnessing to their faith as they encounter new life in love of Jesus.

This week's *advent*ure begins as Mary concludes her journey to Bethlehem, births God's new life, and chooses to silently ponder all these events in her heart. I can barely imagine what it could have been like for Mary to travel so far for the birthing of her child so that the scriptures could be fulfilled. Would you and I travel so far, simply for the love of God? The joy of holding her child, I imagine, overwhelmed her heart. I imagine her gazing with the soft eyes of God's love upon the miraculous new life with which God has gifted her, while at the same time she sees the Divine presence reflected in Jesus' own eyes for the first time—that is a picture of hope, love, joy, and peace.

A companion story of excitement, courage, devotion, and exuber-ant joy, all of which lead to a new way of life—a life filled with peace—is also shared in Luke 2. The shepherds were routinely going about their normal daily duties when God's powerful whisper burst forth. They heard angels singing of God's amazing gift of love birthed into human-ity in the humble stable of a busy town. They went with haste to gaze upon Jesus and personally encounter him. No excuses were given, no fears held them captive. They simply knew in the deepest part of their spirit that God was urging them to experience an awe-inspiring act of Divine love. I imagine such a close-up and personal encounter with Jesus anchored the shepherds with great peace as they moved around from grazing field to grazing field across the years and gave amazing testimony to the arrival of God's Peaceable Kingdom birthed in a stable.

Hundreds of years later, during the earliest centuries of Christianity, earnest seekers of Jesus also sought the Divine whisper of God to lead their lives. This time, however, the men and women did not trek to the city looking for a stable. Instead they sought retreat in the barren land of the wilderness and desert. These men and women lived austere lives of simplicity, striving to cast from their hearts any barriers, resistances, and prideful ego that kept them from truly growing in intimate relationship with God. These men and women are known as the desert mothers and fathers. Many other people from the cities came to the desert to learn from these courageous spiritual fathers and mothers. These desert mothers and fathers who mentored others in the faith were called *ammas* and *abbas*, fitting names, because many other seekers of faith sojourned out in the desert to be discipled under their spiritual guidance; they looked up to them for wisdom and guidance, as children would look to their biological mothers and fathers for guidance. These desert *ammas* and *abbas* wrote extensively of their experience living the descending, ego-shedding way of life toward a transforming love relationship with Jesus. We are fortunate some of their wisdom writings have been salvaged for us to read. It is these sayings of the desert *ammas* and *abbas*, the witness of the shepherds, and Mary's stability of faith that guide us as we reflect on peace and usher in the Peaceable Kingdom with the lighting of the Christ candle this week. As you pray while reading, writing your mandala, and imagining God's Divine whisper, may you too be ignited by the Holy Spirit and impassioned to new possibilities of Christ's life at Christmas.

Your Inward Journey

Just as with Mary, this week we ponder how God has been present to you, whispering to your heart during this Advent *advent*ure. What wisdom has been arising within you during this season? Like the shepherds, you have opportunity to give witness to the ways in which God's whisper has empowered you to respond. With whom do you share your witness of faith, inspiring others to make a personal commitment in love of Jesus? Together with the desert *abbas* and *ammas*, the invitation to be consumed with the power and passionate love of God, which ignites our hearts with the Pentecostal fire of the Holy Spirit, comes to us this week. On Christmas Eve, when the Christ candle is lit, this passion of God finds expression in the stillness of the night as the mysterious birthing of God's new life dawns into our external circumstances of life and with inward holiness of Divine power and energy. Are you ready to receive the gifts of Jesus' new birth?

This week, I invite you to take a day to pause and review your pictorial journal and consider how God has been whispering and filling the God-shaped empty space within you throughout this Advent season on this daily retreat. Where and how have you experienced God's presence during this time of preparation and expectant waiting? Contemplate the effect of emotions and the now current landscape of your heart. What, if anything, has shifted within your attitude, emotions, and posture of your heart since you started this Advent *advent*ure? It is through these slight transformations of heart, as you integrate the virtues of Jesus into daily living, that the power of God's Divine whisper shapes your inward nature to become more like Jesus. Together we venture into the *advent*ure of this Christmas week. May God's Word gift you with holy surprises of Jesus' resurrected presence, bringing new possibilities for peace as you sojourn in prayer through these days.

THE FOURTH SUNDAY OF ADVENT:
A CREATIVE ARTS PRAYER PRACTICE

Meditative Movement: The Spirit Is Gifted with the Body!

I am awe-inspired by God's choice to love humanity in such a magnificent way through bearing the child Jesus (John 3:16). Jesus was fully human, born of Mary, and fully Divine, conceived by the holy presence of God. As beautiful as the soul is, for the soul to have fullness of expression on earth the soul needs a body. The body is the mode of expression for the soul, whether through thought, emotion, talking, reading, serving, or physical touch and movement. The body *is* the soul's outward voice. It is through the body that human beings are able to connect with one another. Soul-deep heart expression is born through the body as we speak our stories and listen to one another, providing opportunity to experience the miracle of God's shared presence among us. It is only through the body that folks are able to work for peace and justice, nourishing the body and feeding the souls of others, making way for God's Kingdom to come upon earth as it is in heaven.

This week is the final approach to Bethlehem. In Bethlehem we find not only the soul-deep desire to stand in awe of what God has done in the birth of Jesus, but also the invitation to humble ourselves by becoming a place for Christ to erode the darkness of our inward nature as God renovates our interior posture for daily living. In the birthplace of Jesus, we find the invitation to become a Bethlehem. Dancer, poet, and spiritual director Betsey Beckman captured this calling to integrate body and soul by becoming a Bethlehem in "So Longs My Soul":

> The soul wants to sing;
> the soul wants to dance;
> the soul wants to explode with color
>> to sit in silence,
>> to reach out in longing
>> to leap like a deer
>> to dress itself in feathers
>> to feel the beat of the drum!
>
> The soul wants a body
> so it can kick up its heels.
> The soul wants a wide, wide skirt
> to wear while it swings and sashays
> all the way down the aisles!
>
> The soul wants to know
> how mercy feels in the bones,
>> in the breath releasing
>> in the soft surrender of fear
> when love takes over
> and all shame, all shadows
> are washed away.
>
> The soul wants to feel the awe
> of a song rising up
> while the dancer

becomes the music,
becomes the meditation.
The soul wants to be the dancer
dancing for us all!

The soul wants to embody
the deep prayers,
rising up from the earth like incense;
the soul wants to become mercy,
to be a balm
for hearts that hurt—
become an embrace
for pain, for poverty, for punishment.

The soul wants a body so it can
be a Bethlehem—
be the place where all that is big
and wide and wonderful,
can put flesh on,
can be born among us into this world,
into this humble humanity.

The soul wants to fly with wild ribbons
rising on the wings of hope.

The soul wants to know you,
God, who soars over time,
who dives deeper than space,
here, now, in our midst,
dancing through us
in this moment, this place
where we are steeped in your mercy,
and so become balm for the world—
souls brimming over with beauty,
moving with your ancient mystery.
Amen![1]

The soul wants and needs a body for fullness of expression and life. The wonders this week are:

- ⊕ How is your body a Bethlehem, that marvelous space for nurturing, holding, birthing, and expressing the virtues of the holy presence of Jesus (hope, love, joy, peace)?
- ⊕ Through what actions, passions, loves, and desires does the risen Christ seek to be born anew through you this week?
- ⊕ How will this new birth of Jesus within your heart bear witness to the Peaceable Kingdom of God coming upon this earth?
- ⊕ How does integration of inward and outward thoughts and actions become the unique ability of individuals to bear the light of God as peace within interpersonal and communal relationships?

To help discern clarity for these wonders, you will experience the creative arts practice of meditative movement, the dance of the soul. I first encountered prayerful meditative movement through the practice of hand dancing at SoulFeast, a spiritual formation conference.[2] As I gave my heart and soul voice through bodily movement, from the first movements I knew union of body and soul and was smitten with a new way of expressing love of God in prayer. There was an immense sense of unity and peaceful connection with God. It touched my heart so deeply that after that experience I began seeking out more ways of movement and prayer. During my search for soul expression from movement, I came upon *Awakening the Creative Spirit: Bringing the Arts to Spiritual Direction* by Christine Valters Paintner and Betsey Beckman. Exercises with prayer posture and hand dancing from this book have inspired some of this week's prayer practices. My search for soul expression continued, and ultimately I have found greatest expression of my soul through the body with my deep love of ballroom dancing!

Don't panic at the words "movement" or "dancing." I encourage you not to become resistant or disparaging of your abilities just because of these words. The exercises for this week's creative expression are very simple movements, and no full-body dancing is involved. Even with varying abilities or mobility, you can pray these meditative movements. You can practice this form of prayer from a chair if you like. These very simple movements engage heart, mind, and body. They are about giving free expression to your spirit in the safety of your sacred space and letting your spirit soar on the wings of God's soul dance.[3]

The Challenges of Meditative Movement

It is interesting to notice what resistance rises when we are asked to do something new. Over the course of this retreat we have looked at feelings and thoughts that deter us from fully embracing the new birthing of Jesus' four virtues of the Advent wreath into our lives. Dance and movement of body are activities with which many folks are uncomfortable. We often do not think of the body as a spiritual partner in deepening and expanding our imagination and awareness of God's presence. Other than bowing your head or raising your hands in praise, the body is not used for prayer on a routine basis. As a result, it may feel awkward to use your body for prayer. You may be embarrassed, not wanting anyone to "catch you in the act" of movement and prayer. You may be captured by the thought, *What if I look silly?*

As we enter this last week of retreat, arriving in Bethlehem and hearing the invitation to become a place for the Divine birth, pause to consider what holds you back from the fullness of the soul's expression. Does fear have you bound, preventing you from venturing out and experimenting with new things? Could there be voices from your past, critics of your abilities who keep you from trying new forms of expression, causing you to believe that you cannot do it … so why try? Or have you found a sense of security in maintaining the order of things around and within you, so as to justify an excuse for not stepping further into the dance of faith?

If you are experiencing resistance to meditative movement, consider the current landscape of your soul. Would it be helpful to express your resistance in a mandala before entering into the movement practices? Resistances are often great learning tools for expanding desire and prayer of the heart. When you are ready, embrace any remaining resistance, placing it under your blessing as you begin this week's creative prayer practice, and experience the joy when union of soul and body bring expression from inward spiritual formation to outward action as you become a Bethlehem. To place any resistance under blessing is to embrace the hesitancy in your mind's eye, then ask God to shine through this weakness so that it may turn from something that keeps us from God to something that draws us closer to God.

The intent of this week's creative arts experience is for you simply to notice the prayer that wells up within as you move your body in prayer, with the hope and anticipation of experiencing God's presence. There is no expectation of anyone to become a professional dancer.

Practicing Meditative Movement

Plan at least thirty minutes for this prayer practice.

On this fourth Sunday of Advent, you will be expressing your soul through movement. This will be experienced either through expression of a circumstance of life that is stuck in your prayerful heart or through listening to music that captures your attention.

There are three distinct prayers for the practice of meditative movement: (1) posture and prayer; (2) the hand dance; and (3) the hand dance challenge. Don't be overwhelmed with the three options today. These meditative movements are little short practices; each one takes only as long as the instrumental music lasts. Generally a song lasts two to four minutes. You may choose to journal or write a mandala after each experience, or you may desire to practice all three and then create your mandala. Please notice the energy of your spirit upon completion of each movement and proceed in a way that is most nourishing for your soul.

To begin, take a few deep cleansing breaths as you prepare for your first experience of meditative movement. Breathe in slowly, drawing the Spirit of God into your awareness. Let God's Spirit fill your lungs with the creative possibility of God's presence. Slowly exhale all resistance and busyness from your day, leaving space for God to fill your heart and imagination. Release any indifference or resistance within you, allowing your heart to experience the allure of God's love, drawing you into deepened prayer as you begin your prayer movements. You will want to take this centering time in preparation for each of the meditative movement prayer practices for this week.

As you begin these prayer practices, offer a prayer anointing your sacred space. Bring to your consciousness the possibility and expectation that in this space you will hear God's whispers to your heart through these practices of prayerful meditative movement. You may use this prayer or one of your own as you begin today's prayer practice:

I come this day, Jesus, with deep desire in my heart. I come seeking to become a Bethlehem, a birthing place for you through expression of my soul. Anoint my posture and prayers. Unite my body, mind, and spirit as I seek to embrace the fullness of my unique being and become more closely shaped into your image. You alone have knit me together in your secret places. You know the deepest desires of my heart. Open the way this day to let all resistance fade away, and let me become a vessel for your new birthing. May your holy surprises fill me and lead me into all my movements throughout this week, so that I may be mindful of the gift you have given my spirit through my precious body. Amen.

Posture and Prayer

Have you ever watched the nightly news and been caught in the heart with grief, hope, sorrow, or joy? One night, while I was watching the news, my heart was captivated in compassion for eleven children who were on a field trip from school to see a science exhibit. An experiment as part of the display went very wrong. It exploded into a burst of flame. The flames shot across the room and burned several of the children. The grief and pain in their cries on the news report tore through my heart. My spirit immediately went to unspoken prayer for these children. But was there more? Was there an even deeper connection my prayer could have made with the surprise, fear, pain, and suffering of these children? An intentional body posture can bring us into solidarity with those who are suffering anxiety, anguish, oppression, injustice, illness, and a whole host of sorrows and grief. What was it like for those children escaping from flames in fear? Is there a body posture that could symbolize the feelings of these children? Maybe a posture on your hands and knees, crawling as fast as you can to escape the flames. Or possibly holding still, frozen in terror, would unify your heart in solidarity with the children's emotions as this tragedy exploded before them.

To use posture as a means of prayer assists the spirit in expressing prayer.[4] The body can express thanksgiving, healing, joy, hope, humility, and the emotion of the situation or person you are praying for in a way that mental prayer alone cannot. Think back to the children and the science exhibit: crouching, stepping backward, and shielding your eyes or raising your hands in terror, or cowering in the corner wide-eyed and looking for escape may strike a prayer deep within your soul in solidarity with their suffering.

For this creative arts prayer practice, you will strike two postures (one posture at a time, of course).

- ⊕ Strike a pose that depicts for you the anguish of those suffering or of those who are ill and in need of healing.
  - ❖ While holding this pose, think of a specific circumstance or person who at this very moment is living through this heavyhearted experience.
  - ❖ Notice the increase or decrease of energy within you and the feelings that arise as you hold this posture.
  - ❖ As you continue to hold this pose, offer a prayer of solidarity with those you have named in the struggle.
  - ❖ When you have finished praying, relax your pose.
  - ❖ Take a few cleansing breaths of Spirit before moving to the next prayer posture.
- ⊕ Strike a pose that is joy-filled, humbled, and filled with thanksgiving and gratitude.
  - ❖ Stay in this posture for a time, basking in the energy and presence of God.
  - ❖ While holding this pose, think of the *same* specific circumstance or person who at this very moment is living through a heavyhearted experience. Let the amazing feelings and prayer of this joy-filled posture before God radiate light, love, and healing upon the person or circumstance that you held in the first posture of prayer.
  - ❖ When you are ready, physically lean forward to pick up all those you have been in prayer with, bringing them into an embrace, crossing your arms over your heart as you offer your prayer to God.

Hand Dance

For this prayer experience you will need a single selection of instrumental music that you can listen to while sitting in your sacred space. You may have a favorite instrumental piece, or you may desire music you have not heard before to gain even greater insights from God's wordless whispers. If you have access to the Internet, there is a variety of music selections at http://musicbrito.com/music.html for your listening pleasure. Type this

link into your browser, then scroll down and click on the most appeal-
ing music selection. You may want to try this prayer movement with a
variety of rhythms and differing styles of music. You may need to experiment with several selections of music before one speaks to your heart and
encourages your hand to move in prayer. As a warm-up to hand dancing,
author Betsey Beckman suggests practicing some hand movements prior
to the prayer activity, or simply move your hand: first fast, then slow,
jerky and smooth, up and down, flowing and staccato.[5]

For this experience, once you select your music:

- Center yourself into a comfortable position in your sacred space
  with your hands free.
- Begin your music selection.
- Move one hand in a dance to the movements of the music.
- Let your soul voice expression through these movements to the
  music.
- When the music finishes, simply rest your hand in a prayerful
  posture, and offer thanksgiving to God for this soulful expression of your inward being.

The Hand Dance Challenge

Because the expression of the soul longs to be shared with others, this challenge invites another person into your sacred space as a witness to your
hand dance. The challenge of this exercise is to follow all of the instructions for the hand dance prayer while another person is physically present before you to witness God's wordless expression through your hand
dance. This act of intimately sharing the expression of your soul is inspiring
to both the hand dancer and the witness beholding the beauty of the dance.
As we draw closer to God, we are drawn closer to one another.

To assist in these meditative movement prayers, I have provided a
few thoughtful questions to stir the imagination and expand awareness
of God's presence:

- How does God invite you into this the dance of the soul through
  movement?
- What is it about the prayer posture, hand dance, and/or the
  hand dance challenge that captivates your heart's attention?

⊕ How do you imagine what you are most drawn to during this time of meditative movement could be God's voice whispering a wooing love song to your heart?

⊕ What is God saying to you through these exercises?

⊕ When did you feel in solidarity with the other, or when did spontaneous joy rise within you, giving way to peace?

⊕ How will you ponder all of these experiences in your heart, just as Mary did?

❧ *Your Mandala: Listening Beyond Words for the Power of a Divine Whisper*

The creation of your mandala is the daily retreat throughout this devotional book. It takes intentional time, focus, and prayer to allow God to silence all distractions of heart and create your mandala. From your prayerful meditative movement, consider how the landscape of your heart has shifted. What feelings, thoughts, and wordless wonders could your spirit be experiencing? No need to try to articulate these wordless insights of God's powerful whisper; simply creating marks and colors on the page can give them expression. I invite you to draw your empty mandala circle as a symbol of the God-shaped emptiness within your soul, which desires to experience Jesus' new Christmas birthing. How can these movement prayers open the way within you for new attitudes, feelings, thoughts to be created? As you fill the circle with colorful expression, notice how God's gift of Jesus' new life is rising within you. What new insights have you gained as you focus on receiving Jesus this final week of Advent? As you look back over your pictorial journal of mandalas from this retreat, how has God's wordless whisper and power come to you as Christmas Day dawns?

Gather your tools of illumination: journal, pen, sketch pad, and colored pencils. Come into God's presence and settle yourself into your sacred space. As you gaze at the beauty of the empty space, ponder God's possibilities.

⊕ If you would like some thoughts to consider as you begin the creation of your mandala, you may choose to consider:

✦ What color represents the feeling of your spirit after prayerful meditative movement?

- ❁ How have hand dancing and prayer postures inspired your spirit?
- ❁ What sensations, thoughts, energies, emotions arise within you as you notice the activity of God's presence and invitation to you through meditative movement?
- ❁ What colors best express these energies and emotions?
- ❁ As you let the Word of God write your reflections through drawing your mandala, consider abstract expression, concrete images, or a mixture of both in the creation of your mandala.

When you have completed your mandala, offer a silent prayer of thanksgiving to God for new insights and wonders as you glean greater wisdom, preparing for Jesus' expectant birth this week.

Special Considerations for Christmas Week

I've provided devotionals for Monday and Tuesday of this week, as well as for Christmas Eve, Christmas Day, and the days following Christmas. If there are more than two weekdays before Christmas Eve, I suggest revisiting prayer practices that resonated with you, that you might like to go deeper with.

- ❁ Try a *lectio divina* practice, using a scripture passage that caught your attention on a previous day in your Advent journey. Guidelines for this practice can be found on pages 21–22.
- ❁ Try an *audio divina* practice, using a fresh selection from http://musicbrito.com/music.html—or try searching "instrumental" on www.soundcloud.com. Guidelines for this practice can be found on pages 81–84.
- ❁ Try a *visio divina* practice, using an image that has captured your heart this Advent season, perhaps from a Christmas card or magazine. Guidelines for this practice can be found on pages 46–49.

I also realize some years there may be several days between Christmas and the first Saturday after Christmas, when you'll use the Saturday Sabbath practice. As you resume your normal daily routines, use these unstructured days to begin a new rhythm of devotion that will lead you into the new year as laid out in the epilogue.

Created in the Image

Luke 2:1–5

> What the Fathers [and Mothers of the desert] sought most of all
> was their own true self, in Christ. And in order to do this, they had
> to reject completely the false, formal self, fabricated under social
> compulsion in "the world." They sought a way to God that was
> uncharted and freely chosen, not inherited from others who had
> mapped it out beforehand. They sought a God whom they alone
> could find, not one who was "given" in a set, stereotyped form by
> somebody else.[6]

You are unique! Even if you are a twin, there is not another person
upon this earth who thinks, feels, prays, desires, anticipates, experiences all of life the way that you do. Each one of us is uniquely created
by God. We are formed in that secret womb where the mystery of God
breathes deeply and knits us together with the potential of blossoming
into the fullness of God's life and desires within us. Remember, the historic definition of Christian spiritual formation is being inwardly shaped
to become more like Christ so that others in relationship with us and
throughout the world can notice and claim the love of Jesus.

    This process of being created more intentionally into the fullness
of the divine image of God is the hope, joy, and greatest desire of the
spiritual journey. This is what the desert *abbas* and *ammas* sought as they
ventured out into arid lands. It was there they came face to face with
their own demons of doubt, worry, anxiety, and fears. In the desert
they could no longer rely on their learned skills, intellectual assets, and
social status. The *abbas* and *ammas* of the desert learned deep within the
core of their beings to rely solely upon God, trusting that God is always
present. They claimed a deep, beyond-words knowing that God *does*
whisper to the heart. By allowing the power of this Divine whisper to

transform their inner self, their lives most nearly reflected divine virtues and the power of God's likeness in all earthly interactions.

As I consider the journey for Mary from annunciation to being
the bearer of God's very presence, the babe lying in the manger, I am
amazed at the amount of traveling she did. First her journey to her
cousin's house, and presumably back home again, or maybe from Elizabeth's she continued on to Bethlehem to tell Joseph the news of Jesus'
impending birth. Then perhaps together they journeyed back to Nazareth. It is from there in Nazareth that our scripture for today comes:

> In those days a decree went out from Emperor Augustus that all the
> world should be registered. This was the first registration and was
> taken while Quirinius was governor of Syria. All went to their own
> towns to be registered. Joseph also went from the town of Nazareth
> in Galilee to Judea, to the city of David called Bethlehem, because
> he was descended from the house and family of David. He went to
> be registered with Mary, to whom he was engaged and who was
> expecting a child.
>   Luke 2:1–5

This Advent retreat has been a journey of the heart and soul. It is one
that invites us to follow the example of the *abbas* and *ammas*, to seek our
own true self in Christ. Today you are invited to pause on your journey. Take intentional prayer time to review where this Advent journey
has taken you thus far. This review of prayerful reflection will follow
the form of the ancient prayer practice from Saint Ignatius called daily
examen.[7]

One way to increase conscious awareness of silent interior spiritual
movement is through the practice of daily examen. The intent of this
practice is to consciously notice how God was present and active during daily life. I liken daily examen to an archeologist's work. Just as the
archeologist intentionally excavates the earth for hidden treasure, so
the spiritual seeker excavates the heart and soul for the hidden treasures
of God's whispering presence.

Today is a reflective day. It is a day of listening beyond the surface
with daily examen. Take out your pictorial journal and any written
reflections you have created during this retreat time. These will be your

tools for examen. The question you will bring to this intentional exca-
vation is, "Is there more within this picture to be revealed to me than
I have yet noticed?" As you review your journal, your inner eye of the
heart and the wisdom of God will assist you in searching out the hidden
treasures of God that you may not yet have noticed.

Begin at the beginning of your journal and gaze upon it with the
eyes and heart of God. Remember, gazing with God's soft eyes is
letting go of judgmental, critical, and analytical thoughts and seeing
beyond the surface to the interior heart of your creation. For each entry
ponder these examen questions:

- How do I see God's consolation (God's presence and activity)?
- How do I notice God's desolation (God's absence and mystery)?

Your Mandala: Listening Beyond Words for the Power of a Divine Whisper

Gather your tools of illumination: journal, pen, sketch pad, and colored
pencils. Come into God's presence and settle yourself into your sacred
space. Upon your sketch pad prayerfully draw your sacred circle for
the creation of your mandala for today. As you gaze at the beauty of the
empty space, ponder God's possibilities.

- Pause. Center yourself by breathing deeply of God's infilling
  Spirit, letting go of all resistances and negativity within your
  heart.
- To begin, read Luke 1:26–56 and 2:1–5, and ponder Mary's
  journey. Imagine when she may have noticed desolation and
  consolation on her journey.
- When you are ready, turn your attention to your own journey
  through your pictorial expression of mandalas, and begin examen of your Advent journey thus far.
- Pray for eyes to notice God's Word present beyond the surface presentation, and ask for openness to receive all that God
  desires to reveal to you.
- During your time of examen, please make note of any consolation and desolation you have experienced during this season.

- ⊕ Following this prayer of examen, let the colors of your spirit flow into the mandala as you begin to draw, considering: How has God anointed your interior posture and prayer?
- ⊕ As you let the Word of God write your reflections in the drawing of your mandala, ponder the hope of Advent's dawning.
  - ✤ What colors are you drawn to?
  - ✤ Consider abstract expression, concrete images, or a mixture of both in the creation of your mandala.
  - ✤ How does the choice of colors reflect your beyond-words knowing of God's Word whispering to your inward being at this stage of your Advent journey?

I encourage you to strive to create a mandala for each devotional reflection. This pictorial journey of reflection beyond words will awaken new possibility through God's wooing whispers as you listen for the advent of God's call this holy season.

Sit back and receive the anointing as the dawning of God's new birth becomes reality in your life. Enjoy the creative expression of God. If creating a mandala for today fails to inspire your heart, consider writing a journal entry, poem, or prayer to express your rumination on God's transforming whispers giving guidance for your truest self to fully embrace life.

Upon completion of your mandala, offer a silent prayer of gratitude in humility for the dawning of insights, wisdom, and wonders of God's Word whispered to you as you continue your pilgrimage to becoming a Bethlehem.

Treasures to Ponder

Luke 2:15–20

> But Mary treasured all these words and pondered them in her heart.
> The shepherds returned, glorifying and praising God for all they had
> heard and seen, as it had been told them.
> Luke 2:19–20

I like the word "ponder." It draws me into deeper thought. It causes
me to hold the subject of my thinking very gently and with deep love.
Holding it gently means without casting judgment and not becoming
attached to certain outcomes that I would wish for. For me, to ponder
means to embrace something in my heart without expectation from the
object of my thinking. Pondering becomes prayer as God lovingly gazes
upon the subject of my thought. To ponder takes interior intentionality. It requires both my mind and my heart to focus upon God and
what I am pondering. It slows the pace of thought and mind as it lays a
foundation for future thoughts and actions.

Mary has had a miraculous nine months! This *adven*ture of God-life
forming within her has left her with an intention for the future. Just
imagine how these words from the shepherds may have resounded in
Mary's heart and soul, anchoring her life: "To you is born this day in the
city of David a Savior, who is the Messiah, the Lord" (Luke 2:11). Did
these words cause her questions? Possibly. Being told that her son would
be "the Messiah, the Lord" could have confirmed for Mary again the
whisper of God's action and creative power. These words may have held
her heart fast in faith, as she trusted that God can and does do miraculous
things as God's new life is birthed within humanity. Would these words
also come to mind as she stood at the foot of Jesus' cross? Probably.

God's Word resounding in the heart and soul provide a stable foundation for life. Mary knew the essence of stability of heart. "Stability is saying

'yes' to God's will for me in the place where I believe God has placed me and with the task I believe God has given me to do."[8] The treasure of words that Mary pondered gave strength and courage to the mother of the one creating and reconciling humankind to God. Jesus becomes the new way, redeeming imperfect humanity to God's perfect love.

I ponder those first few hours or days after Jesus' birth. Did Mary and Joseph have the peace and quiet needed to recover from labor and delivery? How were they able to "tune out" the noise of the bustling streets of Bethlehem and pause in the awesome newness of God's presence among them? What secret whispers did Mary and Joseph share with one another as they marveled at the miracle of new life? What prayers did they offer as they gazed down at this beautiful babe?

Today is about pondering and remaining in the stability of Jesus' new Christmas birthing. The prayer practice for today is the discipline of silence. The discipline of silence is sometimes difficult in the haste of Christmastide, with family feastings and gatherings, with visits or cleaning up after friends have taken leave and returned to normal routines.

I remember when I was expecting my first child. Such joy filled my soul at the thought of being her mom. I often found myself just sitting on the rocking loveseat, whispering tender words and singing simple songs of love to my soon-to-be-born child. One day, when I was truly enjoying the silence of the moment in anticipation and expectation of birthing my daughter, the doorbell rang. A teenager was on the other side of the door. I no longer remember what the teen needed, but I clearly remember her shocked surprise at the quiet and stillness of my home. That is when the teen confessed to me her grave uneasiness with silence. "Too much time to remember and think," she said.

There are many folks today who are not comfortable with silence. If a person finds him- or herself alone with time to spare, often the time is filled with noise. Either the television or music is turned on to waft through the sounds of silence. People do not like silence for many reasons. Some are hoping the noise will drive out unwanted memories and thoughts, as with the teenager who rang the doorbell. Others simply don't like feeling so alone in the stillness of the quiet.

Unfortunately, silence has also been used poorly, as some folks tend to wield silence as a weapon. These are the folks who give other individuals or groups of individuals the "silent treatment." This passive-aggressive behavior of manipulating others into or out of relationships and situations in life is unhealthy and harmful to the souls of all involved. Some justify this silent "shunning" of the other as a means of keeping the peace or avoiding conflict. Others make excuses for using silence as a weapon to withhold love within relationships, to get what they want. Whatever the intent, silence used as avoidance of conversation in relationship is unhealthy and hurtful, and it diminishes soulful connection with God.

Mary turned to silence in a very different and holistic, healthy way. Mary's silence was for pondering and treasuring the words of the shepherds in her heart. This silent pondering created deep union and intimate relationship with God. It is this kind of silence we seek with God today in our spiritual practice of silence.

To begin the practice of silence, it may be necessary to shed some of the urgent and pressing needs of the day. When we seek silence in union and prayer with God, we must first quiet the thoughts of our minds. When the mind wanders to a thought as you are trying to still it, simply glance at the thought in your mind and then return to your focal point of silencing the heart. Techniques for entering silence are suggested in today's practice. There are numerous prayer techniques for quieting the mind and focusing attention upon God. One way is to create a mantra, a six- to eight-syllable phrase that you repeat audibly in your mind to focus on God. The ancient "Jesus Prayer" is an example of a centering mantra. The Jesus Prayer simply calls upon God's power and presence to focus the heart and mind: "Lord Jesus Christ, Son of God, have mercy upon me, a sinner." If this is too churchy, you can easily create a personal mantra by praying a six- to eight-syllable phrase over and over in your mind. Other examples of mantra prayers may be simply repeating the name "Jesus" or "God," or perhaps:

"Jesus, empower me to live your love."
"Creator of life, quiet my heart."

Another technique used to quiet the heart and mind into silence and listening to God is the technique you have been using throughout this Advent retreat. It is the rhythmic technique of coloring. The motion of the crayon slowly moving back and forth draws the heart and mind to stillness and silence. Today as you prepare your mandala, maybe it is simply a technique of drawing that pulls you into silent awareness of God. If you would like, repeat a mantra or your special name for God in your mind to focus your heart into creative listening. The intent of this day is to provide space and time for you to ponder the new gifts of God's birthing within your life.

❧ *Your Mandala: Listening Beyond Words for the Power of a Divine Whisper*

Gather your tools of illumination: journal, pen, sketch pad, and colored pencils. Come into God's presence and settle yourself into your sacred space. Upon your sketch pad prayerfully draw your sacred circle for the creation of your mandala for today. As you gaze at the beauty of the empty space, ponder God's possibilities.

- ⊕ Pause. Center yourself by breathing deeply of God's infilling Spirit, letting go of all resistances and negativity within your heart.
- ⊕ Reread Luke 2:15–20, highlighting particularly verses 19 and 20, and ponder how God speaks to you this day.
- ⊕ Let the colors of your spirit flow into the mandala as you begin to draw, considering:
    - ✤ How has God been present to you in and through this Advent pilgrimage?
    - ✤ How can God's whispered wooing love song that you have heard be shared with others?
- ⊕ Or you may choose to simply rest in silence as you color without intentional thought or design in mind.
- ⊕ As you let the Word of God write your reflections in the drawing of your mandala, consider:
    - ✤ What colors are you drawn to?
    - ✤ Consider abstract expression, concrete images, or a mixture of both in the creation of your mandala.
    - ✤ How does the choice of colors reflect your inward experience of God's holy birthing that shapes your life with Jesus' love to live the virtues of hope, joy, love, and peace?

I encourage you to strive to create a mandala for each devotional reflection. This pictorial journey of reflection beyond words will awaken new possibility through God's wooing whispers as you listen for the power of God's call this holy season.

Sit back and receive the anointing as the dawning of God's new birth becomes reality in your life. Enjoy the creative expression of God. If creating a mandala for today fails to inspire your heart, consider writing a journal entry, poem, or prayer to express how you are at home in God's heart.

Upon completion of your mandala, offer a silent prayer of gratitude for the gift of new life known in your life because of Jesus' birth.

An Invitation to the Manger

Isaiah 9:2
Luke 2:8–16

I was outside the other evening with my dog, Sophie. It was a beautiful, snow-covered silent night. The moonlit ground shone bright as day. The stillness of the air held its breath with expectation as the silent sound of snowflakes gently falling to the ground cascaded into a dizzying array of beauty. My heart and soul were transported to a night long ago. It was to be a night like none other for the shepherds as they gazed skyward and as the mystery of God's angelic chorus rang through the stillness.

Tonight the whispers of invitation are given to turn completely in total abandonment and with full attentiveness of soul to listening. Tonight in the stillness of the dark and wintry sky, God's powerful whisper woos the heart to notice the light penetrating the darkness.

> The people who walked in darkness
> have seen a great light;
> those who lived in a land of deep darkness—
> on them light has shined.
> Isaiah 9:2

Tonight with the fullness of abandon and joy, we surrender in gentle release our fears, resistances, and doubts to the impossible dream. The inner hearing of the heart listens like the shepherds of long ago who gazed into the unknown tomorrow as they heard the Divine whisper:

> "Do not be afraid; for see—I am bringing you good news of great
> joy for all the people."
> Luke 2:10b

Tonight the wooing whispers of God's love sweep over us and seep beyond the surface into a depth of knowing within the hidden mystery of the soul as the Word of God touches our most inward being. It is not just one lone thought or one very small whisper that comes from God, but as our confidence builds and discernment of truly hearing God's voice awakens the heart, the gentle whisper turns into a full chorus.

> "And suddenly there was with the angel a multitude of the heavenly
>   host,
> praising God and saying,
> 'Glory to God in the highest heaven,
> and on earth peace among those whom he favors!'"
>   Luke 2:13–14

Tonight, for us, just as for the shepherds, response is called forth. When soul-deep hearing and interior knowing happen, the necessary response is a shifting of outward and inward posture.

> "Let us go now to Bethlehem and see this thing that has taken place,
> which the Lord has made known to us."
> So they went with haste and found Mary and Joseph,
> and the child lying in the manger.
>   Luke 2:15b–16

Today's reflection is about listening with full expectation. It is surrendering to the final release of attachments, fears, and resistance and with the fullness of God's energy and passionate love causing the soul to run with haste in your heart to the manger. This full release is standing unafraid in God's mystery. It is trusting in God's preferred future, even as the human gaze of realism and logic may look upon a circumstance that seems impossible. Full release in the mystery of God trusts the plans God has for us regardless of which outcome becomes reality. We face with full intention both the logical human realism of situation and circumstance *and*, at the same time, lean into the mystery of God. Trusting the promise of God for good and not evil (Jeremiah 29:11) is *the* moment of possibility when we become bearers of God's mysterious new birthing. Even though we *may prefer* one outcome over the other, with the grace of God's mystery and new birth as our focal point of heart, as Julian of Norwich says, "All shall be well."[9]

If you are still struggling with standing in the mystery and experiencing God's steadiness through all circumstances of life, you may desire to enter into your browser "All Shall Be Well—History Is Ever Ours for the Reliving" or the link www.youtube.com/watch?v=hzyxFJquI6U. This is a musical selection that has a drone or a steadfast underlying note, while the melody has movements both fast and slow. This music helps me experience the foundation of God's steadfast love, while the melody dances with movements of life. This music gives expression to the soulfulness of the spiritual life and is a good selection to practice a two-handed hand dance. With your left hand, hold steady with the sound and movement of God while you move your right hand through the different musical movements of life. Notice how God's steady presence is in and through all movements of this prayer exercise as an exclamation point of how God is a steady presence and source of power and energy through all of life.

Your Mandala: Listening Beyond Words for the Power of a Divine Whisper

Gather your tools of illumination: journal, pen, sketch pad, and colored pencils. Come into God's presence and settle yourself into your sacred space. Upon your sketch pad prayerfully draw your sacred circle for the creation of your mandala for today. As you gaze at the beauty of the empty space, ponder God's possibilities.

- ⊕ Pause. Center yourself by breathing deeply of God's infilling Spirit, letting go of all resistances and negativity within your heart.
- ⊕ Please read Luke 2:8–16.
- ⊕ Let the colors of your spirit flow into the mandala as you run with spiritual haste and expectation to the manger.
  - ❖ What is that like for you to "run with haste" to Jesus? What emotion arises within as you gaze at the infant Messiah?
  - ❖ How is God present to you and in and through you?
  - ❖ What do you imagine God whispering to your heart?
- ⊕ As you let the Word of God write your reflections in the drawing of your mandala, ponder the hope of Advent's dawning:

❖ What colors are you drawn to?

❖ Consider abstract expression, concrete images, or a mixture of both in the creation of your mandala.

❖ How does the choice of colors reflect your choices on the spiritual path at this stage on your Advent journey?

I encourage you to strive to create a mandala for each devotional reflection. This pictorial journey of reflection beyond words will awaken new possibility through God's wooing whispers as you listen for the advent of God's call this holy season.

Sit back and receive the anointing as the dawning of God's new birth becomes reality in your life. Enjoy the creative expression of God. If creating a mandala for today fails to inspire your heart, consider writing a journal entry, poem, or prayer to express how God is inviting you to the manger this night and what your experience is like.

Upon completion of your mandala, offer a silent prayer of gratitude in humility for the persistent presence of God in the midst of humanity, for with God, nothing is impossible.

Away in the Manger ... at Home in the Heart

Luke 2:10–11
John 1:1–4, 14–17

> But the angel said to them, "Do not be afraid; for see—I am bringing you good news of great joy for all the people: to you is born this day in the city of David a Savior, who is the Messiah, the Lord."
>
> Luke 2:10–11

To you this day in Bethlehem a child is born! A Son of the Most High is given. This miracle of Divine birthing is not tucked away in the historical archives "lying in a manger." Today *you* become a Bethlehem, the flesh-and-blood home where the mystery of God's Divine presence will speak a Word and birth new possibility. By the whisper of a Word, the most improbable virginal new thing within the secret interior spiritual womb of your life may awaken.

Today we enter fully into the mystery of the unknown as the Word becomes flesh and dwells among us. We, much like the desert *abbas* and *ammas*, become bearers of the light of Christ for the world.

> These simple men [and women] who lived their lives out to a good old age among the rocks and sands only did so because they had come into the desert to be themselves, their *ordinary* selves, and to forget a world that divided them from themselves.... The Coptic hermits, who left the world as though escaping from a wreck, did not merely intend to save themselves. They knew that they were helpless to do any good for others as long as they floundered about in the wreckage. But once they got a foothold on solid ground, things were different. Then they had not only the power but even the obligation to pull the whole world to safety after them.[10]

Like the ancient societal culture of the desert *abbas* and *ammas*, with lust, greed, wars, jealousies, and injustices, the twenty-first-century believer finds him- or herself in a world ravaged with strife and violence. These conflicting events and the constant fast pace of the North American culture cause a divide to occur between the most authentic God-self soul and the roles we get caught up in living to keep up with all the details of daily life. Temptations to live under cultural domination of success are constantly pushing in upon us. For the dwellers of modern day, the manger always reflects the glory of the cross and the unleashing of the Holy Spirit. It is through the indwelling of the Holy Spirit, the Word—that creative Word of God that whispered in the very beginning and became Incarnate this very day long ago—that you and I are gifted with the reality of becoming Christ-bearers in the world. It is in becoming God-bearers that we find and live from the most authentic self as created in the image of the One who made us. It is here the fullness of the Advent wreath shines brightly as the virtues of Jesus' hope, love, joy, and peace become the guiding principles of life.

> In the beginning was the Word, and the Word was with God, and the Word was God. He was in the beginning with God. All things came into being through him, and without him not one thing came into being. What has come into being in him was life, and the life was the light of all people. The light shines in the darkness, and the darkness did not overcome it....
>
> And the Word became flesh and lived among us, and we have seen his glory, the glory as of a father's only son, full of grace and truth. (John testified to him and cried out, "This was he of whom I said, 'He who comes after me ranks ahead of me because he was before me.'") From his fullness we have all received, grace upon grace. The law indeed was given through Moses; grace and truth came through Jesus Christ.
>
> John 1:1–4, 14–17

The gift of God's creative Word that called each one into being is swept into our heart this day like the rush of breath of God's Holy Spirit. Truly at home in the heart of God, filled with the presence of Divine life and breath, we are called to incarnation. We are invited to be the body, the vessel of God's very presence. We become the embrace for wounded friends, the words of grace for the heartbroken, encouragement and love for those who are the subjects of our greatest relationships.

Today may you become a Bethlehem as Divine love is birthed into your life.

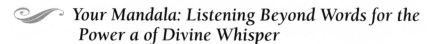

Your Mandala: Listening Beyond Words for the Power a of Divine Whisper

Gather your tools of illumination: journal, pen, sketch pad, and colored pencils. Come into God's presence and settle yourself into your sacred space. Upon your sketch pad prayerfully draw your sacred circle for the creation of your mandala for today. As you gaze at the beauty of the empty space, ponder God's possibilities.

- ⊕ Pause. Center yourself by breathing deeply of God's infilling Spirit, letting go of all resistances and negativity within your heart.
- ⊕ Please read and ponder prayerfully Luke 2:10–11 and John 1:1–4, 14–17.
- ⊕ Let the colors of your spirit flow into the mandala as you begin to draw, considering: How are you becoming this day a Bethlehem for Jesus' power, energy, and new birth?
- ⊕ As you let the Word of God write your reflections in the drawing of your mandala, ponder the joy of this day, as Jesus' new birth of power, energy, and new possibilities dawns in your life.
  - ✤ What colors are you drawn to?
  - ✤ Consider abstract expression, concrete images, or a mixture of both in the creation of your mandala.
  - ✤ How does the choice of colors reflect your experience of coming to the manger and kneeling before the Christ child?

I encourage you to strive to create a mandala for each devotional reflection. This pictorial journey of reflection beyond words will awaken new possibility through God's wooing whispers as you listen for the advent of God's call this holy season.

Sit back and receive the anointing as the dawning of God's new birth becomes reality in your life. Enjoy the creative expression of God. If creating a mandala for today fails to inspire your heart, consider writing a journal entry, poem, or prayer to express soul-deep joy for the gift of God's creative Word whispered into new life within your life.

Upon completion of your mandala, offer a silent prayer of gratitude in humility for the opportunity to be a Bethlehem for God's new life and love to live in you and flow through you to the world.

Ignited in Love

Matthew 2

> Abbot Lot came to Abbot Joseph and said: Father, according as I am able, I keep my little rule and my little fast, my prayer, meditation and contemplative silence; and according as I am able I strive to cleanse my heart of thoughts: now what more should I do? The elder rose up in reply and stretched out his hands to heaven, and his fingers became like ten lamps of fire. He said: Why not be totally changed into fire?[11]

As we come near the end of our Advent retreat, the wonder crosses my mind: How has your life been transformed by this time of retreat? Will others notice a gentling of your soul? When you find yourself in the next difficult circumstance that stretches your faith beyond where you have been, will the pictorial journey of this retreat assist you in anchoring your heart and soul even more deeply in God's presence?

The above story from the desert fathers is one that calls to me. It invites my spirit to seek God so that I can, by the grace of God's presence, become even more formed into my truest self as created in my beginning. The question "Why not be totally changed into fire?" hangs with holiness in the air—the air that was filled just days ago with the melody ringing through the church rafters "There's a Song in the Air."[12] Could it be that we are invited to be fire, invited and called by God to be folks living lives filled with the passion and love of God's holy presence?

And the journey continues. First we hear of the wise men, more folks who come seeking to encounter the living presence of God. Like the wise men, many current-day faithful people come seeking the presence of God by participating in times of retreat. This retreat time of leaving the habitual routines and rat race of daily life provides for a time of setting yourself apart for silence, contemplation, and meditation. These mountaintop experiences are events that may be remembered for a lifetime. The wonder of integration pokes its way into consciousness. How does the retreat time anchor our daily lives? Does it make a difference in our daily choices, relationships, and conversations?

Beyond the shepherds and the wise men who sought Jesus, the journey continued as Mary and Joseph encountered the reality of counterculturalism by living peace amid the chaos of the world. Herod, however, was freaking out in fear. He felt his attachment to power and leadership were threatened by the one child. Herod set a plan in motion to squelch the living light of love.

So our journey also continues ... I am reminded of another song. It is an old familiar song, one you may have known since earliest childhood. And yet the words are timeless and the message is imperative: "This little light of mine, I'm gonna let it shine."[13]

As this Christmas season unfolds in our lives and the light of Jesus' birth glows within, around, and through us, a few wonders cross my mind:

- ⊕ How will you and I let the passion of this retreat ignite into the fullness of God's light as we share the presence of Christmas with others?
- ⊕ What *does* it mean to share the light of Jesus' birth?
- ⊕ Has this retreat influenced you in a way that could enrich the lives of others?
- ⊕ How *will* this pilgrimage through the Advent season make a difference in your daily routines and the choices you make?

∽ *Your Mandala: Listening Beyond Words for the Power of a Divine Whisper*

Gather your tools of illumination: journal, pen, sketch pad, and colored pencils. Come into God's presence and settle yourself into your sacred space. Upon your sketch pad prayerfully draw your sacred circle for the creation of your mandala for today. As you gaze at the beauty of the empty space, ponder God's possibilities.

- ⊕ Pause. Center yourself by breathing deeply of God's infilling Spirit, letting go of all resistances and negativity within your heart.
- ⊕ Let the colors of your spirit flow into the mandala as you begin to draw, considering:
  - ✤ How will you share the hope, joy, love, and peace of the Advent season with others? Name how you will do this sharing. Make a covenant with yourself to actually do this!
  - ✤ As you think of sharing the fruits of your retreat time with others, consider the various levels of relationships you have: personal, interpersonal, and within communities with whom you can share the light and passion of Jesus' love. Where is God calling you to be a witness of Christmas peace and love?
- ⊕ As you let the Word of God write your reflections in the drawing of your mandala:
  - ✤ What colors are you drawn to?
  - ✤ Consider abstract expression, concrete images, or a mixture of both in the creation of your mandala.
  - ✤ How does the choice of colors reflect your passionate covenantal love for Jesus?

I encourage you to strive to create a mandala for each devotional reflection. This pictorial journey of reflection beyond words will awaken new possibility through God's wooing whispers as you listen for the power of God's call this holy season.

Sit back and receive the anointing as the dawning of God's new birth becomes reality in your life. Enjoy the creative expression of God. If creating a mandala for today fails to inspire your heart, consider writing a journal entry, poem, or prayer to express how God invites you to be fully enflamed with Divine love.

Conclude your time of reflection and creative prayer by offering this or another prayer of your choosing to close your time of retreat:

Holy God, Holy One, Holy Three. Thank you for companions who have accompanied me on this pilgrimage. I am truly humbled by your love poured out for us and for all your people through the birth of Jesus. Anoint each one that has been on this monthlong retreat so that this time may become an anchor in our lives as we live into your new possibilities. We love you. We trust into the mystery of your holy presence. Ignite my life so that I may continue to dream impossible dreams and live your resurrection reality into this coming new year. Amen.

Saturday Sabbath

This day is your day to rest. Today is a day of celebration! We have journeyed to Bethlehem and back to the reality of life. In fact, we did more than journey to Bethlehem; we have become a Bethlehem, that glorious body where the living Holy Spirit of God comes alive within our heart and lives outward through our words and deeds. The stillness of the silent night rings of truth and holiness in our most inward parts as we find peace and restoration within and beyond our heart into the community of Jesus. The Advent wreath is complete; the Christ candle has shown one more step toward the Peaceable Kingdom as our intentionality seeks to love God, love self, and love others with the power of a Divine life whispered within us.

Let your spirit settle deeply into the mystery of Divine birthing. Maybe you want to dance, take a winter hike, or gaze up at the starlit sky. The mystery of God's love welling up within humanity is truly a gift to be pondered and delighted in. How will you offer special attention to God today? How will you say thank you for the astonishing way in which Jesus has loved into your life during these past four weeks? To whom will you run with haste and share insights from your spiritual journey of heart-forming love? Today on the silent Sabbath you are free to celebrate God's depth of love by whatever means most deeply touched your heart during this retreat. Was it the creative prayer practice of icon gazing, *audio divina*, or *visio divina* while praying with a video clip? Or maybe meditative movement captured your heart as you posed in solidarity with the pain and joy of others? Is there some Christmas music just awaiting your prayer to dance with your soul? However God rejuvenated, cultivated, and loved you during this expectant season of Divine beauty, celebrate today!

Today claim your belovedness of God. Know that the most authentic and unique you is exactly the strong and courageous person Jesus longs to live through you. Let the living presence of God rejoice with your spirit as your spirit dances freely to the rhythm and beat of the song of Love birthed at Christmas. Be well, my friend, as the Peaceable Kingdom dawns new hope and possibility in the midst of your daily life. Rest well, my dear companions, for the journey does not end at Christmas. The *adven*ture into the new year is only beginning.

The *Adventure* into the New Year

The Foundation for Daily Devotion

*The hours of time pass swiftly by; the dawning
of each new day brings possibility for the
everyday birthing of God within life.*

Dear companions on this ever-deepening way to new life in Christ, *now* is the time the fun of everyday life begins!

As this new year's *advent*ure begins, notice the interior landscape of your heart. Is there relief that the structure of the book is completed and you have a sense of accomplishment? Does guilt weigh upon you, because even with all good intention time slipped away and completion of retreat slid into the abysses of lostness and incompletion? Is there a slight tug of sorrow pulling upon your heart at finishing this Advent retreat? Have you slipped back into the routines of daily living, with the spiritual highs of the Advent and Christmas season simply dissipating into a distant memory?

Often at the close of any retreat participants are on a spiritual high as they enter back into the daily tasks of life. Soon with the rhythm of life's ebb and flow the retreat becomes just a fleeting memory of a time when God's presence was most powerfully felt in life. We want the effects to last, but time spent away on retreat may or may not influence the next days, weeks, months, and years of life. A bishop once told me that he saw many leaders within the church going away on retreats and other deeply formational and inspiring events, but when he looked at the skills of the leader, the ministries of the church … alas, it appeared the holy moments of retreat had little to no lasting impact upon everyday life and leadership. This is for me a very sad statement on the current status of the church.

It is my prayer that with this epilogue you will find ways to intentionally integrate your experience from this daily devotional and retreat during Advent into the power and presence of each day of this new year. It is not enough just to go to the mountaintop during the holy seasons. God's wooing whisper of love *is* power for birthing new resurrection possibilities in daily living 365 days a year. God comes to us in the ordinary and mundane of life just as certainly as God's presence is known through the extraordinary seasons of retreat.

The intent of this epilogue is to explore ways of intentionally integrating the high holy moments of faith experienced on retreat into a lasting influence and foundation for life as you leap into the days and weeks ahead in this new year. There are several ways of incorporating profound experiences of God's presence into your everyday life. I certainly do not fool myself into believing I know them all or have the "correct formula for prayerful success." Yet the Spirit of God is miraculous, alive, and working in the hidden mystery of life. May these thoughts encourage desire, pierce imagination, and increase daily devotion.

You may have already felt an interior shifting of posture and attitude within yourself as you experienced the prayer practices from the past month of Advent retreating. The question becomes, "How do I remain in this new place of interior heart in the heat of the stressors and the angst of daily life?" Now the spiritual practices are where "the rubber hits the road" of everyday life. To get your imagination stirring on how to build this new year upon the foundation of your Advent experience, read on! You are the expert of your soul. You know the nuances of God's presence breathing deeply within your life. So follow your heart's lead as God guides you into this new *advent*ure.

Marking the Dawn of Advent Birthing Year-Round

From dusk to dawn the light
Penetrates the darkness, and in
The stillness of the night
The Light beams on.

Creation of Covenant's Renewing Presence

How do you pray to mark events in your life? When my children received their driver's licenses, the family celebrated. When birthdays come around every year, there is the traditional cake and ice cream, family gatherings, and the often off-key rendition of "Happy Birthday" sung before the candles are blown out on the cake. For graduations, anniversaries, birthings, and homecomings of new babies, parties are given and folks join in the celebration of the feast.

We mark high holy days through the Christian year with special worship events: Easter, Palm Sunday, Maundy Thursday, and Good Friday, to name just a few. Each of these special worship celebrations commemorates and celebrates a formational time in the Christian faith that has forever changed our relationship with God. What about within our personal lives? How are we to celebrate and remember, to name and forever claim the high moments of retreat and influential inspiring formation of God in our lives? What marker, what celebration, what tradition could deliberately write our intent upon the heart and make covenant of our commitment to live faithfully into the next days and weeks of life? How *do* you pray and *whom do you gather* to note and celebrate the shifts of the landscape of your heart as you become more nearly formed into the image of Christ for the sake of others?

Will there be an intentional gathering of the saints of your community to celebrate the interior deepening of your heart in love for God? If so, how often would you desire to review and renew your commitment? Would a monthly reading of a personal prayer entice your stability and steadfast commitment to a year of intentional formation? Could a conference phone call with your spiritual kinship bless you as you bless them in the sharing of prayers and commitment and covenant desire to do justice, love others, and walk gently into the next humble circumstance of life?

I am an oblate in Saint Brigid of Kildare Methodist-Benedictine Monastery.[1] This dispersed community of believers is geographically scattered around the nation. Yet together we pray the Daily Offices of prayer, as we are able, renew our covenant to the community annually, and celebrate the feast days of those who have gone before us in passionate love and faithfulness to God. Through the mysterious connection of Christ and with the help of free conference calling, we are united in Christ as our spirits are edified and God is glorified. The big "Woo-hoo! Yippee!" on a call when a novice joins the oblation of community pierces the hearts of all who love God.

There are numerous covenant renewal prayers found on the Internet. One such prayer, written in 1780 by John Wesley, the founder of Methodism, still grounds many in the intentional and surrendering love to God's service for actively living life:

A Covenant Prayer in the Wesleyan Tradition

I am no longer my own, but thine.
Put me to what thou wilt, rank me with whom thou wilt.
Put me to doing, put me to suffering.
Let me be employed for thee or laid aside for thee,
exalted for thee or brought low for thee.
Let me be full, let me be empty.
Let me have all things, let me have nothing.
I freely and heartily yield all things to thy pleasure and disposal.
And now, O glorious and blessed God, Father, Son, and Holy Spirit,
thou art mine, and I am thine.
So be it.
And the covenant which I have made on earth,
let it be ratified in heaven.
Amen.[2]

This is an old-fashioned prayer and may not speak earnestly to the desires of your heart. Yet when considered with the heart, you can hear the whisper of God and the desire of the pray-er to lovingly follow God's way in life. Pause your reading of the epilogue to spend intentional time this day asking God to show you how to pray your intention to faithful living this year. You may use the structure below to discern the creation of your covenant renewal prayer as you seek to remember the highlights from your Advent retreat into everyday living throughout the year. Or you may choose to write a prayer more closely aligned with your heart's hope and desire for remaining in intimate love and faith with Jesus this year, using the phrases from the Lord's Prayer.

❦ *Creating a Covenant Renewal Prayer*

Please do not limit your imagination and prayer with these thoughts. The intent of the reflective questions below is to encourage heart and soul in communion with God to co-create a prayer that will best anchor your heart in commitment before God, self, and others this coming year.

Consider:

- ❀ How will you intentionally move into even more intimacy with Jesus this coming year? *Our Father, who art in heaven, hallowed be Thy name.*
- ❀ How will you surrender your agenda; your priority of time, desires, and passions as God shapes your interior landscape this year? *Thy Kingdom come, Thy will be done.*
- ❀ What practices or disciplines of heart, mind, and body are you invited to pick up this season? *Give us this day, our daily bread.*
- ❀ How will you re-center your life when other events, relation-ships, ministries, and situations threaten to abscond with your good desires for spiritual formation? *Forgive us our trespasses as we forgive those who trespass against us.*
- ❀ What attachments will you lay down today, tomorrow, or next month to open even more time and space within your heart to notice God's presence and power within your life? *Lead us not into temptation, but deliver us from evil.*
- ❀ With whom and how will you celebrate the joy of God's heart beating within your heart and God's breath filling your days this year? *For Thine is the kingdom, and the power, and the glory forever and ever. Amen.*

May it be so! Now that a covenant renewal prayer has swept into your heart, the question arises: How often will it be prayed?

The Rhythm for Life

The sea's pulse beats, waves wash upon the shore.
The katydids clamor to be heard,
singing in rhythm to eve's twilight sky.
The wind of the willow sweeps color across the sky.
Life designed from beginning to end
Hope secure
Passion blooms and love abides.

Implementing a Plan of Prayer in Action

While I was writing this book, I moved to the country. Owls take flight and hunt at night. The groundhog plays the day away, while the majestic deer hold heads up high. What I notice about nature is the unrelenting order of life. Each bug, each wisp of wind, each momentary stillness all point to the majesty of Divine order. There is a certain harmony, a balance innately known throughout creation that holds to the rhythm of God's divinely ordered life. Order is everywhere. Not just within nature, but human life is steeped in order. School buses run like clockwork, with each driver sticking tightly to the schedule. Daily commuters travel the roadways, scurrying to work and home again. The days pass steadily through the rhythm of dark and light as they meld into the season of planting and harvest, the heat of summer and the chill of winter.

With the formal ending of the rhythm of daily devotion and this Advent retreating, how will life find order? What balance is called forth from the hidden depths of heart to create a harmony of devotion throughout this new year? This entire Advent journey was based upon listening with the inner ear of your heart and noticing the interior nudges and the gentle Word of God whispered in life. Now comes the time to intentionally put spiritual muscle into all ordinary days of life and to bring order to life each day through a commitment to live focused on the heartbeat of God.

One of the ways of anchoring life and finding stability in God during all seasons and experiences of life is setting a guide or a rule to follow for faith formation and paying attention to God. A plan of prayer action and accountability is vital for the holistic health of body, mind,

and spirit. Historically, when an individual or a community sought stability of heart in faith before God, they vowed to follow what is known
as a "rule of life."

Around 500 CE, Saint Benedict wrote one of the most widely
practiced "Rule of Life" documents. Followers of this Rule can be found
today, just as there were years ago. Believers both individually and in
community seek order in spiritual formation, and this rich historic legacy
of prayer provides rhythmic harmony for a life focused on prayer and
work. Saint Benedict had a deep heart of love for God and longed for
others to experience the same steadfastness of God's presence in their
lives. He sought to encourage the brothers of the monastery in solitary,
relational, and community practices of edification in spiritual formation.
Benedict wrote the Rule of Life so that believers could have a written way
of disciplining their life to notice even the slightest nuances of God's interior nudging. He realized that without intentional effort and awareness,
the spiritual life could easily fade into lukewarm mediocrity. Benedict did
not want his brothers to lag in zeal and passion for God.

The word "rule" is sometimes a stumbling block for modern folks.
For contemporary ears, "rule" implies a right and wrong way of doing
things, with reward and punishment. The intent of Benedict's Rule was
not reward and punishment. His Rule was a guide for assisting folks in
finding a rhythm of prayer, work, and study that would nourish the soul
through deepened relationship with and love for Jesus, as well as keep
order within the monastery. With the Rule, Benedict specified hours of
prayer, scripture for each time of prayer, a mandate for silence, and a
call for hospitality as the primary focus of Benedictine brothers.

Today is a call to intentionality for everyday living as you enter into
this new year. It is time to explore creative vision and implement prayer
in action for a personal Rule of Life. What will your rhythm of prayer
and practice of attentive listening for God's gentle whisper be on a daily
basis through this new year? How will you weave together the practice
of holy listening and work? Will work overshadow times of prayer? Will
prayer become another "have to do" on a list of chores, until your spirit
is parched and screaming for another extended retreat time? As you
reflect upon the insights and experiences from your daily Advent retreat,
how could God be nudging you toward intentional rhythm and practice

of prayer as foundation and stability for daily life? What do you imagine a sustainable rule could be for your life this next year?

✍ *Rule of Life: Designing an Intentional Plan of Spiritual Formation*

A Rule of Life, or an intentional plan for spiritual formation, can be as detailed or as general as you are most comfortable with. When I was first introduced to the concept of creating a Rule of Life for my life, I was given a very structured outline to complete. This outline touched on every area of human life, from exercise and financial and relational resources to worship, service, and prayer practices. I dutifully completed the contracted Rule of Life that was before me, and I have to admit, it felt like a noose around my spirit! I felt so tied to all of the "have to" disciplines of my rule that I quickly gave it up.

I tell this story not to discourage you from this practice, but to encourage you to *simplify* and *focus* on the most important aspects you would like to carry with you through this new year as practice for deepening your experience of God's presence in life. Choosing just one item, such as reading a biography of a saint or a biblical character each month, is one great discipline to take into the new year. Maybe the creative arts of writing, drawing, or playing music are important disciplines to your soul. To assist in discerning what practices may excite your soul, look through your pictorial journal from the Advent daily retreat and see if you notice a pattern of any particular exercises or prayer practices that truly ignited your heart in passionate love and expectation for God. The days that gave you the greatest insight and awakening of spirit may be guiding clues for practices that you may want to continue into the months ahead.

The creation of an intentional plan of spiritual formation doesn't even have to include specific practices but may outline a rhythm of time and a routine of attentiveness that you would like to practice through this coming year. For example, I had a bishop at one point who set before leaders within the church a Rule of Life, or intentional goals for spiritual life. His Rule of Life was three simple intentional goals:

1. Pray one hour each day.
2. Take one Sabbath day a month.
3. Go on spiritual retreat for one week a year.

Clearly this is not as complex as the seventy-three chapters of Saint Benedictine's Rule. However, this simple guide offers a rhythm of listening, speaking, discerning, and deepening one's awareness of God in the midst of life and ministry. There are no limits on how you should pray for the hour. The imagination and the likes and dislikes of the pray-er could co-create with God how best to spend the allotted time in prayer. Perhaps an hour of prayer experienced by hiking, canoeing, or walking through the streets of urban blight to notice places of humanity's greatest need would be venues of meaningful prayer. Or the daily hour of prayer could be spent at your computer or with paper and pencil, journaling, composing music, drawing mandalas, or practicing other forms of art. Possibly an hour of silence and solitude reading scripture, listening as the Word of God whispers to the mind and heart, would cause the hour of intentional prayer to soar by.

There are many ways to create intentionality in life by providing a rhythm of prayer and focus. You may have already thought of a few best suited for your lifestyle and prayer preferences. Or you may find what follows to be an igniting spark, lighting the way for intentionality of prayer and work.

As this co-creating with God begins for your personal Rule of Life for this year, please hold a printed copy of your covenant renewal prayer in your hands and keep its words near your heart.

Step 1. Consider the aspects of your covenant renewal prayer as the foundation for your personal Rule of Life.

⊕ How will you specifically and intentionally seek to deepen your passionate love for Jesus? Are there activities that ignite your faith with an excitement that holds you in God's presence during wakeful hours and may even keep you from falling asleep at night? If so, could these active thoughts become points of joy to look forward to participating in on a daily, weekly, monthly, or yearly rhythm for your Rule of Life? (In the next step of creating your Rule of Life, you will think about the time line you would like to use to put these activities or practices into motion and accountability for spiritual maturity. For now, the invitation is to pause and create a listing of your heart's desires that draws your attention and focuses your heart nearer to God's heart.)

⊕ What items of busyness fill your day but do not bring meaning or purpose to your life? Are these items just keeping you busy? Could God be inviting you to surrender some of the busyness to open time and space in your day and within your spirit? Be specific about the items of your day, week, month, or year that do not edify your faith. Begin asking God for clarity on shifting agenda items of busyness into meaningful formation practice.

⊕ God's powerful whisper penetrates all of life. How could God nudge your heart to desire new practices of faith, deepening discipleship and weaving work and prayer together in union with God? Be specific. Could it be more *audio divina* opportunities, *lectio* or *visio divina* prayers, maybe examen, ballroom dancing, hiking, silence? God is whispering to your heart—what practices of prayer entice your spirit?

⊕ What attachments—very good things you deeply love in your life, or not-so-good circumstances—do you have in your life that you cling to for security? Which ones will you lay aside for this season of prayer to make even more spacious opportunity for God while you covenant to practice your Rule of Life? How will you make God a priority each day of this year?

⊕ Create a list of people you would like to celebrate your faith with this year. These could be people you currently know or possibly folks you would like to reach out to and meet. Who will form your community of saints to encourage you on this ever-deepening faith *adven*ture this year?

Step 2. Now that you have completed your prayerful contemplation of how to deepen your spiritual foundation and formation this year, it is time to plan strategies for how to accomplish what your heart desires. Refer to the simple three-step Rule of Life:

1. One hour a day
2. One Sabbath day a month
3. One Sabbath week retreat a year

You may want to make a grid as illustrated to assist in the finalization of your Rule of Life.

Activities	1 hour a day	1 monthly Sabbath day	1 Sabbath week a year

What prayer actions will you place in the spaces on this grid? You may find that for the daily hour of prayer you have a repetitive practice such as praying the Daily Office, reading scripture, journaling, and drawing. Your monthly Sabbath day may be filled with different exciting passions of your heart from your first item of reflection above in step 1. And for the Sabbath week you may have only one or two choices that you will discerningly plan for.

Step 3. When you complete your grid, offer a prayer of thanksgiving to God for this intentional plan of creating a foundation of daily devotion for this coming year. You may not fulfill all of these hopes and dreams of spiritual formation within this year, but modern people are strategic planners in most other arenas of life, so why not aim high as God seeks to shape your life into the most authentic image of Christ you can be!

As we near the end of our time together, let us turn our attention to one final facet for leaning into a new year of interior formation. This final gem of spiritual formation is for me the essence of authentic faithful living by anchoring the advent of *advent*ure through claiming and naming a personal guiding scripture as you live deeply from the watermarking of baptism.

Know Thy Story

"Who am I?"
whispered the mind to the soul.
"Why am I here?"
murmured the heart to the body.
"What is the authentic Word for my life?"

Now is the moment of claiming and naming the solid foundation of faith as personal biblical DNA is discovered and the *advent*ure into the new year is shaped by who we are most authentically created to be by God's design.

Living from Biblical DNA

There are two stories within the Bible that most shape my inward being. One I discovered in my first preaching class at seminary. A friend and I did a dialogical sermon as we jointly reflected upon John 4, the Samaritan woman's story as she encountered Jesus at the well. To begin this sermon we read the dialogue of the text. My friend read the words of Jesus. I read the Samaritan woman's side of the conversation. From that very first reading, I knew beyond any doubt her words were my words.

The journey of discovery for this woman was, and still is, very powerful for me. The courage to converse with Jesus, to question, to doubt, to encourage, and to invite others to discover for themselves "Could this be the Messiah?" gave me a great sigh of relief and steadfast call to ministry.

The sigh of relief came as the pressure lifted from my seminary journey knowing I did not have to have all the answers! The Samaritan woman had a lot of questions, and the progression of her spiritual formation was clear, but she did not have to have all the answers. She simply trusted Jesus in conversation and knew deep within her being that God would guide the way, in conversation, in discovery of faith formation, in relation to others, and most importantly in her deep abiding relationship with Jesus.

This story has been my call to ministry. As the first woman preacher, the Samaritan woman ran to the community and without fear of misunderstanding or rejection excitedly proclaimed the invitation to come and see. The invitation issued was to come and see for themselves the One who opened her heart and mind to greater understanding and experience of God's grace and love. The deeply personal life-changing encounter with Jesus becomes the most prophetic call to resurrection living for community.

The primary focus of my ministry in spiritual formation, retreat, teaching, preaching, Bible study, and church administration, and prayer ministry is simply the invitation to come and see. I seek to open time and space in the busyness of the twenty-first century to invite folks to "come and see" this amazing presence of Jesus, which actively lives within, through, and surrounding humanity and all of creation.

The second biblical story that watermarks my life with the baptismal presence of the living water of Christ also comes from the Gospel of John. Hidden in the seventh chapter of John is a little life-changing phrase that anoints life and commissions humanity into authentic living. It connects us to our baptismal beginnings as God's living water seeps soul deep into humanity, empowering and commissioning us to live as Jesus loves.

> On the last day of the festival, the great day, while Jesus was standing there, he cried out, "Let anyone who is thirsty come to me, and let the one who believes in me drink. As the scripture has said, 'Out of the believer's heart shall flow rivers of living water.'" Now he said this about the Spirit, which believers in him were to receive; for as yet there was no Spirit, because Jesus was not yet glorified.
> John 7:37–39

From the watermarkings of baptism the Holy Spirit empowers life and love as Jesus' living, active presence of life-shaping power is whispered into the world.

This personal logo depicts for me the living presence of Christ's Holy Spirit powerfully present in creation. My biblical DNA with the rivers of living water and the narrative between Jesus and the Samaritan

woman anchors my desire to live and love as one passionately in love with Jesus and companioning others into the discovery of even deeper spiritual formation throughout life. If you look closely at the logo, you will notice the incorrect scripture reference. I have thought of correcting it, but as it is, I always have before me the knowledge that God is still perfecting my life and dearly loves even the most imperfect me.

Now is your time of discovery for the new year. Maybe you already know your biblical DNA, the story that anchors your heart and soul as you live your faith within this world. Or perhaps this is a new thought for you. If you are just coming to an invitation to discover for the first time your biblical DNA, I invite you into a time of discerning prayer as you notice what whispers of God from scripture powerfully catch your heart's attention and inscribe them upon your heart.

Maybe praying through the Bible seeking your biblical DNA will become one of your first activities and prayer practices for your Rule of Life as you enter this new year.

> Live boldly of God throughout this new year!
> Live lightly, my companions.
> Hold gently those whom you love so there is always space for Jesus
>   in the midst of everyday life.
> Live ready to receive and even more ready to give.
> Claim your truest identity as the beloved one of Christ.
> Be well, dear sojourner,
> thanks for companioning me on this *advent*ure of a lifetime.

As you leap into the new year, may these practices bring stability to the weary soul and courage to live life from the watermarking of God's new birth, as you experience the power of the Divine possibility serenading each day of your life with the whisper of love.

Brenda

Leader's Guide

Welcome to the leader's guide for *The Advent of God's Word*. This book's retreat-style format is designed to open the way for small groups to share the presence of God while praying with the pictorial journal each participant has created. The suggestions in this leader's guide may be used for both online and on-site small groups.

Participants will each need:

- ⊕ A copy of *The Advent of God's Word: Listening for the Power of a Divine Whisper*
- ⊕ A pad of drawing paper for the pictorial or written journal
- ⊕ A package of colored pencils or other drawing instruments and any written journal material

The leader will need:

- ⊕ A copy of *The Advent of God's Word: Listening for the Power of a Divine Whisper*
- ⊕ A pad of drawing paper
- ⊕ Access to a television and projector or computer with a live Internet connection
- ⊕ Optional: If a singing bowl or Tibetan bell is available, the leader may desire to have one present. The intent of the singing bowl is to gently strike the wooden mallet on the side of the bowl, igniting the resounding sound of the bowl to ring for a length of time, signaling the participants to transition from one focus to another. This could signal the group to enter into a time of silence, conclude silent prayer, draw the group back together after each creative arts prayer time, or be used at any other time the facilitator desires to draw the group's attention to God's presence.
- ⊕ If the group would like fellowship time following the retreat meeting, create a list of persons who will provide weekly snacks.

The leader will also need to create sacred space for the meeting. This may include creating an altar, lighting a candle, and having instrumental music playing when the guests arrive.

I suggest hosting an orientation at the first Sunday gathering on the first Sunday of Advent. An extra half hour will be needed for the orientation time. Following the orientation and each Sunday thereafter, the Sunday gatherings will be a time of practicing together the Sunday creative arts prayer experience. The purpose and procedures of the book will be explained during the orientation as outlined below. If the leader has funding available and chooses to supply all participant materials, then at the orientation meeting the leader will distribute the book, a drawing pad, and a package of colored pencils to each participant. The leader will then highlight the structure of the material and practice creating a mandala, as explained in the introduction of the book. For each Sunday gathering you will need a computer or a television and projector with Internet access.

Suggested Outline for Orientation

As the participants arrive, greet them and have a brief time of getting to know one another. This may include short introductions by sharing:

 ⊕ Name and what drew them to this book group.
 ⊕ An opening prayer. You may use the prayer below or one of your own.
 ⊕ For online groups, introductions may occur through discussion forum postings or through the use of webcams.

Once introductions are completed, invite participants into a centering time by lighting a candle and beginning with a time of silence to transition from the busyness of the day and to focus attention of heart and mind upon listening for the power of God's presence and whispered word.

The leader/facilitator may say something like the following to assist participants in entering into the silence:

> As we enter into this time of silence, gently release the hustle and bustle of the seasons: Thanksgiving gatherings, decorating for Christmas, shopping, baking, and the everyday normal routines of life.

Slowly breathe in through your nose the refreshing energy and breath of God's Spirit. And gradually and persistently exhale your breath, giving release to all that may push in upon you this day.

Now, rest in this spacious emptiness and let God fill your heart and mind as you invite the Holy Spirit of God to come upon you and swell within you during this time of silent centering and prayer.

Conclude the time of silent centering by praying. The leader may read aloud this prayer or one of their own choosing:

Holy One, Holy Three, as we enter into the Advent season, may your holy presence whisper to our hearts and minds, expanding imagination and piercing the darkness of winter and the hurriedness of the shopping season. Draw us into your presence, surprise us with your mysterious love, birthing new hope and possibilities in the midst of our lives. Knit our hearts together that we may become one heart and one baptism through you, Lord. Grant that as we listen and speak, ponder and pray with one another, we may notice your very presence as we see and hear your words living incarnate within each person. Reveal to us your heart's desire so that our hearts may be prepared and ready to receive your new birthing. We love you and long to experience the joy of Jesus in our midst. Amen.

Turn to a review of the book. Walk participants through the structure of the book, highlighting the desire to increase awareness of God beyond the written words on these pages into paying attention to the interior movement of God and nudges of God's presence. Throughout this daily devotional retreat, participants are invited to notice the quickening of the soul on the inside of one's being as God increases influence and formation within each individual life. The book is designed with two unique features to assist in paying attention to God's wordless power: the weekly Sunday creative arts prayer practices and mandalas.

1. *The weekly Sunday creative arts prayer practices.* Each Sunday, participants will have an opportunity to practice an ancient prayer technique and apply it to current-day living. The creative arts prayer practices are icon gazing, *visio divina*, *audio divina*, and meditative movement. Each creative arts prayer experience will

be practiced in the small-group gathering. If this is an Internet group, then the format will be shifted so that the individuals practice the creative arts prayer ahead of the small-group gathering and scan in their mandalas for sharing with the entire group on a discussion board or through webcam.

2. *Mandalas* (please turn to page 9 for instructions and introduction of the mandala). This ancient prayer circle is one way to move the heart beyond the mental and written words of speech to notice the beyond-word whispers of God's powerful Word.

3. *Clarify any questions,* and then continue with the instructions for the week's creative arts prayer practice. The second, third, and fourth Sundays will begin with the time of silence and centering and then move directly into the reflection time and creative arts prayer practice. To introduce the weekly theme and the biblical or historical companions for the week, the leader will need to read the week's introduction thoroughly before beginning the weekly retreat gathering. Before beginning the weekly creative arts prayer practice, the leader will discuss the introduction and highlight which characters are accompanying participants on the weekly journey. Consider: How does the weekly theme move the participants through a process of spiritual formation during this Advent season? How does each weekly companion exemplify the theme and assist in integrating the theme into your discovery on this Advent *advent*ure?

For complete instructions on each creative arts prayer practice, please read the weekly Sunday devotional and share reflections with the group.

Format for Sunday Gatherings

⊕ Gather with music to center the participants into a prayer posture. The music could be instrumental audio or a music video projected on the screen via Internet connection.

⊕ Welcome and greet participants.

⊕ Center the group through lighting the Christ candle.

    ✦ Introduce three minutes of silence, during which time participants are asked to consider what they may need to

let go of in order to be fully present to God's divine presence (for example: the hectic pace of the day, concerns for
loved ones, joys upon the heart).

✤ During this silence have each participant invite Jesus to
help him or her become fully present to God through this
session, asking for the ears to hear the gentle whispers and
nudges of God's Word through your time together.

✤ Close the silence with a time of spoken prayer. This can
be said by the leader or any member of the class, if the
leader has made arrangements with an individual before the
beginning of the class.

⊕ Review the theme for the week and the weekly companions.

✤ Week one, found on page 1:
  The candle of hope
  Theme—Discerning the landscape of the heart
  Companions—Mary, the mother of Jesus; Zechariah

✤ Week two, found on page 35:
  The candle of love
  Theme—Choice: listening for the transformational
    whisper
  Companions—John the Baptist; Elizabeth, his mother;
    and Saint John of the Cross

✤ Week three, found on page 75:
  The candle of joy
  Theme—Deep joy: listening to the soul's song
  Companions—Mary and Elizabeth

✤ Week four, found on page 113:
  The candle of peace
  Theme—New life springs forth
  Companions—Mary, the shepherds, and the desert
    father and mothers

⊕ Introduce the creative arts prayer practice on the appropriate
page within the body of this book.

✤ First Sunday of Advent: icon gazing, found on page 5.
✤ Second Sunday of Advent: *visio divina*, found on page 42.
✤ Third Sunday of Advent: *audio divina*, found on page 79.

❖ Fourth Sunday of Advent: meditative movement, found on page 118.

  ❊ Give instructions.

  ❊ Ask for clarifying questions.

  ❊ Remind participants that following the practice of the creative arts prayer experience there will be fifteen minutes of silence while folks create their mandalas.

  ❊ Before commencing, speak a prayer anointing this time of prayer.

⊕ Read/review the weekly Sunday theme, companions, and devotional for the appropriate Sunday. Highlight which creative arts prayer practice will be shared during the small-group gathering.

⊕ Invite participants to get comfortable for the creative arts prayer practice.

⊕ Ask participants to take out their drawing pads, colored pencils or other drawing instruments, and any written journal material they will need. This is for silent reflection at the conclusion of the creative arts prayer practice.

⊕ Project the appropriate creative arts prayer practice for the week. This will take at least fifteen minutes to a half hour depending upon the prayer practice for the given week. A half hour for each practice is suggested.

⊕ Without further instruction, ask the group to enter into fifteen minutes of silence while creating their mandalas. For participants who choose not to draw a mandala, have journal paper and pen prepared so they may journal their reflections.

⊕ To bring the group back together after the creative arts prayer practice, gently call participants to attention, or ring a Tibetan bell or singing bowl to gather participants back to community awareness.

⊕ At this point, participants may need a short break to transition from their deep time of prayer. This would be a good moment to share a snack, stretch your legs, and have a restroom break.

⊕ Gather the community back together either through word or with the use of the singing bowl or bell.

⊕ For the second half of the small-group gathering, invite participants to share their wisdom and insights gained from this creative arts prayer practice. If participants are comfortable sharing their mandalas, they may do so one at a time during this section of the small-group time. For those who are not comfortable sharing their mandalas, simply have them speak about the process of their experience of this prayer time. Some possible points to guide the discussion are as follows:

  ✦ Name a specific learning you discovered about listening to God's whispers through this creative arts prayer—for example, how you noticed a felt sense of God during your creative arts prayer practice.

  ✦ Write a prayer of thanksgiving for the time you spent noticing God's presence through this practice.

    ❊ Include what you are most thankful for about the process of the creative arts prayer.

    ❊ Express thankfulness for God's Word that whispered to your heart.

    ❊ Express thankfulness for how this Word of God will shape your posture as you move forward in the season of Advent.

  ✦ What was it like for you to practice this creative arts prayer discipline?

  ✦ How did this experience of creative arts prayer shape your posture of heart as you progress on this Advent journey?

  ✦ After each individual has shared, pause and have a silent or spoken prayer of blessing for that individual. This may include blessing the mandala and the person so that the essence of the mandala (joy, peace, freedom, hope, and so forth depicted in the mandala) may come to reality within the individual's life through this next week as each daily devotion is prayed at home.

⊕ When all have shared, conclude your small-group time by reviewing next steps of this retreat.

  ✦ Highlight participants' "homework" of reading and practicing the mandala exercises for the coming week.

    ❖ Explain the possibilities of the Saturday Sabbath options. These are highlighted at the end of each week.

    ❖ Remind participants when and where you will gather next and who will be bringing snacks, if they are provided.

    ❖ Have participants take home their created mandalas, devotional and retreat books, and colored pencils and drawing pads. Remind them to please bring all of these items back with them next week.

  ⊕ Conclude your gathering time with a blessing benediction.

This small-group format is repeated each week. However, the fourth Sunday, like the first Sunday, is extended by a half hour. On the fourth Sunday the extra half hour follows *after* the completion of the creative arts prayer practice. This final half hour is to send the participants off into the new year creating a foundation of daily retreat and devotion as the epilogue is introduced.

Epilogue—The *Adventure* Continues

This final half hour is for encouragement and instruction for participants to experience the epilogue on their own time. Or if the group desires, a date may be set to return together within the first three weeks of the new year for a three-hour retreat. The intent of the epilogue is to create a foundation of daily devotion for the new year.

    A suggested outline for the concluding half hour is as follows:

    1. Review the three sections of the epilogue:
        a. Creating a personalized covenant renewal prayer
        b. Establishing a Rule of Life
        c. Discerning one's biblical DNA

  2A. If the group decides *not* to gather for a three-hour new year's retreat, then the leader will speak a prayer of blessing for each participant to live out their commitment to a life of daily devotion and prayer throughout the new year as outlined in the epilogue of the book.

  2B. If the group decides to gather for a three-hour new year's retreat, it is encouraged to set the date for this day early in

January. Set up the details of this day now. Get commitments from the participants:

    a. Who will be in attendance at the new year's retreat?

    b. Who will bring snacks and refreshments?

    c. Who will set the altar area and arrange the room setting?

    d. Name the facilitator of this new year's retreat.

    e. Each participant will bring a copy of this book and their drawing pad.

3. Open the new year's retreat with the same format given for the orientation session. However, the beginning prayer should be a prayer of anointing this time for the new year rather than for the Advent season.

4. Divide the three-hour retreat into three sections.

    a. Each hour a new section of the epilogue will be highlighted and experienced.

    b. Each hour of the new year's retreat could be structured as follows:

        i. Ten-minute overview and instruction of the foundational exercise.

        ii. Twenty-five minutes of silent contemplation and completion of the exercise (creating a personalized covenant renewal prayer, establishing a Rule of Life, and discerning personal biblical DNA).

        iii. Twenty minutes of sharing in small groups (or through webcams) personal reflections on the experience of creating covenant renewal prayers, establishing a Rule of Life, and discerning personal biblical DNA.

        iv. Five minutes for closing prayer of this section and transition to the next foundational exercise.

5. At the conclusion of the new year's retreat, the facilitator will offer a prayer of blessing for each participant, anointing him or her with the power of God's Word to keep his or her new year commitments as experienced in this epilogue and empower him or her to live faithfully this commitment of daily devotion and intentional spiritual formation throughout the new year.

For an online new year's retreat time, the group may discern it is most convenient to follow the above three-hour format with webcams or possibly to hold three one-hour webcam sessions. Perhaps discussion forums are the best mode for posting and sharing covenant renewal prayers, Rules of Life, and biblical DNA. Depending on the tools accessible for online small groups, the facilitator will decide the best forum for spiritual formation and sharing into the new year.

Enjoy the *adventure of discovery as Jesus' birthing is experienced within your life and small-group community throughout the Advent season and into the new year!

Notes

Introduction

1. The first time I created a pictorial journal with the use of the mandala was during an online Lenten retreat presented by Christine Valters Paintner, from the Abbey of the Arts: Transformative Living Through Contemplative and Expressive Arts. For more information on this community, please visit http://abbeyofthearts.com.

2. Here is the full quotation: "What else does this craving, and this helplessness, proclaim but that there was once in man a true happiness, of which all that now remains is the empty print and trace? This he tries in vain to fill with everything around him, seeking in things that are not there the help he cannot find in those that are, though none can help, since this infinite abyss can be filled only with an infinite and immutable object; in other words by God himself" (Blaise Pascal, *Pensees*, trans. A. Krailsheimer [New York: Penguin, 1995], 10.148).

3. This phrase comes from the opening line of the Rule of Saint Benedict. Benedict, a lay monk from the sixth century, articulated this call to listen to God's Word whispering within the heart in the Rule of Saint Benedict, which he wrote for those who sought to deepen relationship with Jesus. The Rule begins "Listen carefully, my son [and daughter], to the master's instructions, and attend to them with the ear of your heart." (Rule of Saint Benedict, Prologue, *The Rule of Saint Benedict in English*, trans. Timothy Fry [Collegeville, MN: Liturgical Press, 1982], 15.)

    Benedict was born in Nursia, Italy, in 480 CE, into a wealthy family. The global culture into which he was born was one of turmoil and conflict. There were many warring factions vying for power as the Roman Empire crumbled. He was sent to Rome to study; however, he abandoned his studies because he felt the city of Rome was too corrupt. He did not want to be tempted by all of the drinking and women within the city. He traveled instead to the nearby town of Subiaco. It was in Subiaco that Benedict lived for three years as a hermit and then founded a monastery. He left this area when his life was threatened by a priest who attempted to kill him by poisoning the bread that was blessed for the sacraments. Benedict then moved to Monte Cassino, where, with that community of monks, Benedict wrote his Rule—a set of rules for orderly living for the monks. The primary focus of the Rule of Saint Benedict was on hospitality. The Rule focused on "how to live in relationship with God, self and others." The purpose of the Rule is to "explain how we can live a Christ-centered life with others" (Jane Tomaine, *Saint Benedict's Toolbox: The Nuts and Bolts of Everyday Benedictine Living* [New York: Morehouse, 2005], 21). Other resources on Benedict's Rule for living in community are: Glenn W. Olsen, "The Benedictine Way of Life: Yesterday, Today, and Tomorrow," *Communio* 11 (Spring 1984): 35 (available at www.communio-icr.com/issues); Joan Chittister, *The Rule of Benedict: Insights for the Ages* (New York: Crossroads, 2005); and Kathryn Howard, *Praying with Benedict* (Winona, MN: St. Mary's Press, 1996). The Rule of Saint Benedict can be found in its entirety at www.osb.org/rb/text/toc.html.

Week One

1. The Saint John's Bible at Saint John's Abbey in Collegeville, Minnesota, has been illumined by hand and creates a stunning event as the depictions of God's Word soaks into the viewer's being. Please visit www.saintjohnsabbey.org for complete information on Saint John's Abbey.

2. Anne Broyles, in the introduction to the book of Zechariah from *The Spiritual Formation Bible: Growing in Intimacy with God Through Scripture* (Grand Rapids, MI: Zondervan, 1999), 1259.

Week Two

1. For more information on the movie *It's a Wonderful Life*, see www.filmsite.org/itsa.html.

2. Simply entering "the prodigal son" into your browser will provide several options for your viewing. I found a video created for a church film festival competition by director Casey Bankord, filmed by Alex Meinert, and edited by Dustin Bankord at www.youtube.com/watch?v=nxfdChYCKYA.

3. Meister Eckhart, "The Hope of Loving," in *Love Poems from God: Twelve Sacred Voices from the East and West*, trans. and ed. Daniel Ladinsky (New York: Penguin Compass, 2002), 109.

4. Ibid., 90.

5. A summary of Saint Augustine's theology from the Christian Heritage Institute follows: "Heart bursting with the reality of God, he addresses his manuscript directly to the Lord as one long prayer and meditation—a prayer and meditation that will take him five years to complete. He dips his quill and begins, 'Great are you, O Lord, and greatly to be praised; great is your power, and your wisdom is infinite.' In contrast to God, he muses, what is man? Yet there is a connection between the two. Humans, such a small part of creation and short-lived as they are, still find a need to praise God. In spite of sin, each feels the longing to reach out to his Creator. Why is this? He realizes it is the doing of God. 'You have made us for yourself, and *our hearts are restless until they can find rest in you.*' That line summarizes the theme of Augustine's life and will not be bettered in all the writings that lie ahead of him, in which he will wrestle with the deepest issues of theology." From Dan Graves, "Our Hearts Are Restless," Christian History Institute, www.christianhistoryinstitute. org/incontext/article/augustine.

6. Saint John of the Cross, "The Living Flame of Love," from *The Collected Works of Saint John of the Cross*, trans. Kieran Kavanaugh and Otilio Rodriguez (Washington, DC: ICS Publications, 1991). For enhanced connection you may find the complete text and commentary on this poem for your contemplation by entering the poem's title, "The Living Flame of Love," or the following link into your browser: www.jesus-passion.com/LivingFlameLove.htm.

Week Three

1. Since 2006, Karen, a fellow cofounder with me of Hearts of Fire, has been playing the Native American flute as a prayer practice, allowing the Spirit's breath to flow through her, and she uses it in her ministry of spiritual direction and retreat leading. She tells me she has discovered that playing the flute connects the deep longings of her soul to the Creator's love and cultivates a sense of oneness with all of creation and all time. The pentatonic minor scale to which the flutes are tuned produces a mystical and haunting sound that enters the heart and soul and fills it with beauty

and peace. More recently, several other instruments have found their way into her ministry as well, including the Native American drum, the zither, and the Moyo drum. Receiving her Native American name, Chanwi—Lakota for Moon Willow—has fostered an awareness of the way in which all of her life experiences, including the painful ones, contribute to a sense of wholeness and joy.

2. "The Impossible Dream" was composed by Mitch Leigh, with lyrics by Joe Darion, for the musical *Man of La Mancha* (1965), based on *Don Quixote*, a comedic adventure story, set during the Spanish Inquisition. The song is also featured in the 1972 film *Man of La Mancha*, starring Peter O'Toole.

3. More information about John Wesley's works and life may be found at http://wesley.nnu.edu/john-wesley.

4. Dawn is a registered trademark of Procter & Gamble.

5. From *The Psalms: An Inclusive Language Version Based on the Grail Translation from the Hebrew* (Chicago: GIA Publications, 1986), quoted in *Benedictine Daily Prayer: A Short Breviary*, ed. Maxwell E. Johnson (Collegeville, MN: Liturgical Press, 2005), 1050.

Week Four

1. Betsey Beckman, "So Longs My Soul," in *Awakening the Creative Spirit: Bringing the Arts to Spiritual Direction* by Christine Valters Paintner and Betsey Beckman (New York: Morehouse, 2010), 63–64.

2. SoulFeast is a spiritual formation conference sponsored by the Upper Room and General Board of Discipleship of the United Methodist Church, held at Lake Junaluska, North Carolina.

3. To learn more about meditative movement and creativity in experiencing God's presence, check out Paintner and Beckman, *Awakening the Creative Spirit: Bringing the Arts to Spiritual Direction*.

4. This experience is based on the contribution by Roy DeLeon in Paintner and Beckman, *Awakening the Creative Spirit*, 67. For further exploration of his work, please see DeLeon's book *Praying with the Body: Bringing the Psalms to Life* (Orleans, MA: Paraclete, 2009).

5. Paintner and Beckman, *Awakening the Creative Spirit*, 6.

6. Thomas Merton, *The Wisdom of the Desert* (New York: New Directions, 1970), 4.

7. Indigo Ignatius was born in 1491 to Spanish landowners. He served and was wounded in the Spanish military. During his recovery, he began reading the lives of the saints and was converted to Christianity. While he was recuperating, "through the exercise of his imagination in prayer and meditation, Ignatius soon began to realize that this new spiritual freedom enabled him to move from sin to an experience of God's call" (Barbara Bedolla and Dominic Totaro, "Ignatian Spirituality," in *Spiritual Traditions for the Contemporary Church*, ed. Robin Maas and Gabriel O'Donnell [Nashville: Abingdon, 1990], 173). He wrote the Spiritual Exercises of Saint Ignatius, developed from his own striving for a spiritually disciplined life. He led students through these exercises for deepened awareness of God's presence. Examen of consciousness is one of the steps of these exercises. It involves a review of daily activity that assists one in becoming aware of how God's presence was consciously noticed and when one's attention was not captured by God's activity during daily events. For further information on Saint Ignatius, see http://faculty.georgetown.edu/jod/twayne/aug3.html.

8. Jane Tomaine, *Saint Benedict's Toolbox: The Nuts and Bolts of Everyday Benedictine Living* (Harrisburg, PA: Morehouse, 2005), 47.

9. For further information on the fifteenth-century English anchoress Julian of Norwich, see www.lordsandladies.org/julian-of-norwich.htm.

10. Thomas Merton, *The Wisdom of the Desert*, 25–26. Emphasis mine.

11. Thomas Merton, *The Wisdom of the Desert*, 106.

12. Find versions of this song using http://goo.gl/MufrSd.

13. See www.lyricsmode.com/lyrics/r/religious_music/this_little_light_of_mine.html.

Epilogue

1. For more information on Saint Brigid of Kildare Methodist-Benedictine community, see www.kildaremonastery.com.

2. *The United Methodist Hymnal* (Nashville: United Methodist Publishing House, 1989), 607.

Suggestions for
Further Reading

Christensen, Michael J., ed. *Nouwen Through the Wesleyan/Methodist Lens*. With Rebecca J. Laird. Nashville: Cokesbury, 2015. Includes all volumes of Christensen's Nouwen trilogy: *Spiritual Direction, Discernment,* and *Spiritual Formation*.

De Waal, Esther. *A Life-Giving Way: A Commentary on the Rule of St. Benedict*. Collegeville, MN: Liturgical Press, 1995.

Foster, Richard J. *Celebration of Discipline: The Path to Spiritual Growth*. Rev. ed. San Francisco: HarperSanFranciso, 1998.

Hudson, Trevor. *Holy Spirit: Here and Now*. Nashville: Upper Room, 2012.

Judy, Dwight. *A Quiet Pentecost: Inviting the Spirit into Congregational Life*. Nashville: Upper Room, 2013.

Keller, David. *Desert Banquet: A Year of Wisdom from the Desert Mothers and Fathers*. Collegeville, MN: Liturgical Press, 2011.

Lawrence of the Resurrection [Brother Lawrence]. *The Practice of the Presence of God with Spiritual Maxims*. Compiled by Father Joseph de Beaufort. Grand Rapids, MI: Spire Books, 2005.

Paintner, Christine Valters. *The Artist's Rule: Nurturing Your Creative Soul with Monastic Wisdom*. Notre Dame, IN: Sorin Books, 2011.

———. *Desert Fathers and Mothers: Early Christian Wisdom Sayings—Annotated & Explained*. Woodstock, VT: SkyLight Paths, 2012.

———. *Lectio Divina—The Sacred Art: Transforming Words & Images into Heart-Centered Prayer*. Woodstock, VT: SkyLight Paths, 2011.

———, and Betsey Beckman. *Awakening the Creative Spirit: Bringing the Arts to Spiritual Direction*. New York: Morehouse, 2010.

Palmer, Parker J. *A Hidden Wholeness: The Journey Toward an Undivided Life*. San Francisco: Jossey-Bass, 2004.

Rohr, Richard. *Falling Upward: A Spirituality for the Two Halves of Life*. San Francisco: Jossey-Bass, 2011.

Swan, Laura. *The Forgotten Desert Mothers: Sayings, Lives, and Stories of Early Christian Women*. Mahwah, NJ: Paulist Press, 2001.

Thiele, William. *Monks in the World: Seeking God in a Frantic Culture*. Eugene, OR: Wipf & Stock, 2014.

Thompson, Marjorie J. *Soul Feast: An Invitation to the Christian Spiritual Life*. Rev. ed. Louisville, KY: Westminster John Knox, 2014.

Credits

Inspiration

The Golden Rule and the Games People Play
The Ultimate Strategy for a Meaning-Filled Life
By Rami Shapiro
A guidebook for living a meaning-filled life—using the strategies of game theory and the wisdom of the Golden Rule.
6 x 9, 176 pp, Quality PB, 978-1-59473-598-1 **$16.99**

Deepening Engagement
Essential Wisdom for Listening and Leading with Purpose, Meaning and Joy
By Diane M. Millis, PhD; Foreword by Rob Lehman
A toolkit for community building as well as a resource for personal growth and small group enrichment.
5 x 7¼, 176 pp, Quality PB, 978-1-59473-584-4 **$14.99**

The Rebirthing of God
Christianity's Struggle for New Beginnings
By John Philip Newell
Drawing on modern prophets from East and West, and using the holy island of Iona as an icon of new beginnings, Newell dares us to imagine a new birth from deep within Christianity, a fresh stirring of the Spirit.
6 x 9, 160 pp, HC, 978-1-59473-542-4 **$19.99**

Finding God Beyond Religion: A Guide for Skeptics, Agnostics & Unorthodox Believers Inside & Outside the Church
By Tom Stella; Foreword by The Rev. Canon Marianne Wells Borg
Reinterprets traditional religious teachings central to the Christian faith for people who have outgrown the beliefs and devotional practices that once made sense to them. 6 x 9, 160 pp, Quality PB, 978-1-59473-485-4 **$16.99**

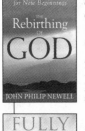

Fully Awake and Truly Alive: Spiritual Practices to Nurture Your Soul
By Rev. Jane E. Vennard; Foreword by Rami Shapiro
Illustrates the joys and frustrations of spiritual practice across religious traditions; provides exercises and meditations to help you become more fully alive.
6 x 9, 208 pp, Quality PB, 978-1-59473-473-1 **$16.99**

Perennial Wisdom for the Spiritually Independent
Sacred Teachings—Annotated & Explained
Annotation by Rami Shapiro; Foreword by Richard Rohr
Weaves sacred texts and teachings from the world's major religions into a coherent exploration of the five core questions at the heart of every religion's search.
5½ x 8½, 336 pp, Quality PB, 978-1-59473-515-8 **$16.99**

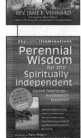

Journeys of Simplicity: Traveling Light with Thomas Merton, Bashō, Edward Abbey, Annie Dillard & Others By Philip Harnden
5 x 7¼, 144 pp, Quality PB, 978-1-59473-181-5 **$12.99**

Saving Civility: 52 Ways to Tame Rude, Crude & Attitude for a Polite Planet
By Sara Hacala 6 x 9, 240 pp, Quality PB, 978-1-59473-314-7 **$16.99**

Spiritually Healthy Divorce: Navigating Disruption with Insight & Hope
By Carolyne Call 6 x 9, 224 pp, Quality PB, 978-1-59473-288-1 **$16.99**

Or phone, fax, mail or email to: SKYLIGHT PATHS Publishing
Sunset Farm Offices, Route 4 • P.O. Box 237 • Woodstock, Vermont 05091
Tel: (802) 457-4000 • Fax: (802) 457-4004 • www.skylightpaths.com
Credit card orders: (800) 962-4544 (8:30AM–5:30PM EST Monday–Friday)
Generous discounts on quantity orders. SATISFACTION GUARANTEED. Prices subject to change.

Sacred Texts—SkyLight Illuminations Series

Offers today's spiritual seeker an enjoyable entry into the great classic texts of the world's spiritual traditions. Each classic is presented in an accessible translation, with facing pages of guided commentary from experts, giving you the keys you need to understand the history, context and meaning of the text.

CHRISTIANITY

The Book of Common Prayer: A Spiritual Treasure Chest—Selections Annotated & Explained
Annotation by The Rev. Canon C. K. Robertson, PhD; Foreword by The Most Rev. Katharine Jefferts Schori; Preface by Archbishop Desmond Tutu
Makes available the riches of this spiritual treasure chest for all who are interested in deepening their life of prayer, building stronger relationships and making a difference in their world. 5½ x 8½, 208 pp, Quality PB, 978-1-59473-524-0 **$16.99**

Celtic Christian Spirituality: Essential Writings—Annotated & Explained
Annotation by Mary C. Earle; Foreword by John Philip Newell
Explores how the writings of this lively tradition embody the gospel.
5½ x 8½, 176 pp, Quality PB, 978-1-59473-302-4 **$16.99**

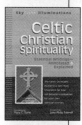

Desert Fathers and Mothers: Early Christian Wisdom Sayings—Annotated & Explained *Annotation by Christine Valters Paintner, PhD*
Opens up wisdom of the desert fathers and mothers for readers with no previous knowledge of Western monasticism and early Christianity.
5½ x 8½, 192 pp, Quality PB, 978-1-59473-373-4 **$16.99**

The End of Days: Essential Selections from Apocalyptic Texts—Annotated & Explained *Annotation by Robert G. Clouse, PhD*
Helps you understand the complex Christian visions of the end of the world.
5½ x 8½, 224 pp, Quality PB, 978-1-59473-170-9 **$16.99**

The Hidden Gospel of Matthew: Annotated & Explained
Translation & Annotation by Ron Miller
Discover the words and events that have the strongest connection to the historical Jesus.
5½ x 8½, 272 pp, Quality PB, 978-1-59473-038-2 **$16.99**

The Imitation of Christ: Selections Annotated & Explained
Annotation by Paul Wesley Chilcote, PhD; By Thomas à Kempis; Adapted from John Wesley's The Christian's Pattern
Let Jesus's example of holiness, humility and purity of heart be a companion on your own spiritual journey.
5½ x 8½, 224 pp, Quality PB, 978-1-59473-434-2 **$16.99**

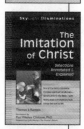

The Infancy Gospels of Jesus: Apocryphal Tales from the Childhoods of Mary and Jesus—Annotated & Explained
Translation & Annotation by Stevan Davies; Foreword by A. Edward Siecienski, PhD
A startling presentation of the early lives of Mary, Jesus and other biblical figures that will amuse and surprise you. 5½ x 8½, 176 pp, Quality PB, 978-1-59473-258-4 **$16.99**

John & Charles Wesley: Selections from Their Writings and Hymns—Annotated & Explained *Annotation by Paul W. Chilcote, PhD*
A unique presentation of the writings of these two inspiring brothers brings together some of the most essential material from their large corpus of work.
5½ x 8½, 288 pp, Quality PB, 978-1-59473-309-3 **$16.99**

Julian of Norwich: Selections from Revelations of Divine Love—Annotated & Explained *Annotation by Mary C. Earle; Foreword by Roberta C. Bondi*
Addresses topics including the infinite nature of God, the life of prayer, God's suffering with us, the eternal and undying life of the soul, the motherhood of Jesus and the motherhood of God and more.
5½ x 8½, 224 pp, Quality PB, 978-1-59473-513-4 **$16.99**

Sacred Texts—continued

The Lost Sayings of Jesus: Teachings from Ancient Christian, Jewish, Gnostic and Islamic Sources—Annotated & Explained
Translation & Annotation by Andrew Phillip Smith; Foreword by Stephan A. Hoeller
Depicts Jesus as a Wisdom teacher who speaks to people of all faiths as a mystic and spiritual master. 5½ x 8½, 240 pp, Quality PB, 978-1-59473-172-3 **$16.99**

Philokalia: The Eastern Christian Spiritual Texts—Selections Annotated & Explained *Annotation by Allyne Smith; Translation by G. E. H. Palmer, Phillip Sherrard and Bishop Kallistos Ware* The first approachable introduction to the wisdom of the Philokalia. 5½ x 8½, 240 pp, Quality PB, 978-1-59473-103-7 **$18.99**

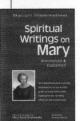

The Sacred Writings of Paul: Selections Annotated & Explained
Translation & Annotation by Ron Miller Leads you into the exciting immediacy of Paul's teachings. 5½ x 8½, 224 pp, Quality PB, 978-1-59473-213-3 **$16.99**

Saint Augustine of Hippo: Selections from *Confessions* and Other Essential Writings—Annotated & Explained
Annotation by Joseph T. Kelley, PhD; Translation by the Augustinian Heritage Institute
Provides insight into the mind and heart of this foundational Christian figure.
5½ x 8½, 272 pp, Quality PB, 978-1-59473-282-9 **$18.99**

Saint Ignatius Loyola—The Spiritual Writings: Selections Annotated & Explained *Annotation by Mark Mossa, SJ* Focuses on the practical mysticism of Ignatius of Loyola. 5½ x 8½, 288 pp, Quality PB, 978-1-59473-301-7 **$18.99**

Sex Texts from the Bible: Selections Annotated & Explained
Translation & Annotation by Teresa J. Hornsby; Foreword by Amy-Jill Levine
Demystifies the Bible's ideas on gender roles, marriage, sexual orientation, virginity, lust and sexual pleasure. 5½ x 8½, 208 pp, Quality PB, 978-1-59473-217-1 **$16.99**

Spiritual Writings on Mary: Annotated & Explained
Annotation by Mary Ford-Grabowsky; Foreword by Andrew Harvey
Examines the role of Mary, the mother of Jesus, as a source of inspiration in history and in life today. 5½ x 8½, 272 pp, Quality PB, 978-1-59473-001-6 **$16.99**

The Way of a Pilgrim: The Jesus Prayer Journey—Annotated & Explained
Translation & Annotation by Gleb Pokrovsky; Foreword by Andrew Harvey A classic of Russian Orthodox spirituality. 5½ x 8½, 160 pp, Illus., Quality PB, 978-1-893361-31-7 **$15.99**

GNOSTICISM

Gnostic Writings on the Soul: Annotated & Explained
Translation & Annotation by Andrew Phillip Smith; Foreword by Stephan A. Hoeller
Reveals the inspiring ways your soul can remember and return to its unique, divine purpose. 5½ x 8½, 144 pp, Quality PB, 978-1-59473-220-1 **$16.99**

The Gospel of Philip: Annotated & Explained
Translation & Annotation by Andrew Phillip Smith; Foreword by Stevan Davies
Reveals otherwise unrecorded sayings of Jesus and fragments of Gnostic mythology.
5½ x 8½, 160 pp, Quality PB, 978-1-59473-111-2 **$16.99**

The Gospel of Thomas: Annotated & Explained
Translation & Annotation by Stevan Davies; Foreword by Andrew Harvey
Sheds new light on the origins of Christianity and portrays Jesus as a wisdom-loving sage.
5½ x 8½, 192 pp, Quality PB, 978-1-893361-45-4 **$16.99**

The Secret Book of John: The Gnostic Gospel—Annotated & Explained
Translation & Annotation by Stevan Davies The most significant and influential text of the ancient Gnostic religion. 5½ x 8½, 208 pp, Quality PB, 978-1-59473-082-5 **$18.99**

See Inspiration for Perennial Wisdom for the Spiritually Independent: Sacred *Teachings—Annotated & Explained*

Spiritual Practice—The Sacred Art of Living Series

Teaching—The Sacred Art: The Joy of Opening Minds & Hearts
By Rev. Jane E. Vennard Explores the elements that make teaching a sacred art, recognizing it as a call to service rather than a job, and a vocation rather than a profession. 5½ x 8½, 160 pp, Quality PB, 978-1-59473-585-1 **$16.99**

Conversation—The Sacred Art: Practicing Presence in an Age of Distraction
By Diane M. Millis, PhD; Foreword by Rev. Tilden Edwards, PhD
5½ x 8½, 192 pp, Quality PB, 978-1-59473-474-8 **$16.99**

Dance—The Sacred Art: The Joy of Movement as a Spiritual Practice
By Cynthia Winton-Henry 5½ x 8½, 224 pp, Quality PB, 978-1-59473-268-3 **$16.99**

Dreaming—The Sacred Art: Incubating, Navigating & Interpreting Sacred Dreams for Spiritual & Personal Growth *By Lori Joan Swick, PhD*
5½ x 8½, 224 pp, Quality PB, 978-1-59473-544-8 **$16.99**

Fly-Fishing—The Sacred Art: Casting a Fly as a Spiritual Practice
By Rabbi Eric Eisenkramer and Rev. Michael Attas, MD; Foreword by Chris Wood, CEO, Trout Unlimited; Preface by Lori Simon, executive director, Casting for Recovery
5½ x 8½, 160 pp, Quality PB, 978-1-59473-299-7 **$16.99**

Giving—The Sacred Art: Creating a Lifestyle of Generosity
By Lauren Tyler Wright 5½ x 8½, 208 pp, Quality PB, 978-1-59473-224-9 **$16.99**

Haiku—The Sacred Art: A Spiritual Practice in Three Lines
By Margaret D. McGee 5½ x 8½, 192 pp, Quality PB, 978-1-59473-269-0 **$16.99**

Hospitality—The Sacred Art: Discovering the Hidden Spiritual Power of Invitation and Welcome *By Rev. Nanette Sawyer; Foreword by Rev. Dirk Ficca*
5½ x 8½, 208 pp, Quality PB, 978-1-59473-228-7 **$16.99**

Labyrinths from the Outside In, 2nd Edition
Walking to Spiritual Insight—A Beginner's Guide *By Rev. Dr. Donna Schaper and Rev. Dr. Carole Ann Camp* 6 x 9, 208 pp, b/w illus. and photos, Quality PB, 978-1-59473-486-1 **$16.99**

Lectio Divina—**The Sacred Art**
Transforming Words & Images into Heart-Centered Prayer
By Christine Valters Paintner, PhD 5½ x 8½, 240 pp, Quality PB, 978-1-59473-300-0 **$16.99**

Pilgrimage—The Sacred Art: Journey to the Center of the Heart
By Dr. Sheryl A. Kujawa-Holbrook 5½ x 8½, 240 pp, Quality PB, 978-1-59473-472-4 **$16.99**

Practicing the Sacred Art of Listening
A Guide to Enrich Your Relationships and Kindle Your Spiritual Life
By Kay Lindahl 8 x 8, 176 pp, Quality PB, 978-1-893361-85-0 **$18.99**

Recovery—The Sacred Art: The Twelve Steps as Spiritual Practice *By Rami Shapiro*
Foreword by Joan Borysenko, PhD 5½ x 8½, 240 pp, Quality PB, 978-1-59473-259-1 **$16.99**

Running—The Sacred Art: Preparing to Practice *By Dr. Warren A. Kay*
Foreword by Kristin Armstrong 5½ x 8½, 160 pp, Quality PB, 978-1-59473-227-0 **$16.99**

The Sacred Art of Chant: Preparing to Practice
By Ana Hernández 5½ x 8½, 192 pp, Quality PB, 978-1-59473-036-8 **$16.99**

The Sacred Art of Fasting: Preparing to Practice
By Thomas Ryan, CSP 5½ x 8½, 192 pp, Quality PB, 978-1-59473-078-8 **$15.99**

The Sacred Art of Forgiveness: Forgiving Ourselves and Others through God's Grace
By Marcia Ford 8 x 8, 176 pp, Quality PB, 978-1-59473-175-4 **$18.99**

The Sacred Art of Listening: Forty Reflections for Cultivating a Spiritual Practice
By Kay Lindahl; Illus. by Amy Schnapper 8 x 8, 160 pp, b/w illus., Quality PB, 978-1-893361-44-7 **$16.99**

The Sacred Art of Lovingkindness: Preparing to Practice
By Rabbi Rami Shapiro; Foreword by Marcia Ford 5½ x 8½, 176 pp, Quality PB, 978-1-59473-151-8 **$16.99**

Spiritual Adventures in the Snow: Skiing & Snowboarding as Renewal for Your Soul
By Dr. Marcia McFee and Rev. Karen Foster; Foreword by Paul Arthur
5½ x 8½, 208 pp, Quality PB, 978-1-59473-270-6 **$16.99**

Thanking & Blessing—The Sacred Art: Spiritual Vitality through Gratefulness
By Jay Marshall, PhD; Foreword by Philip Gulley 5½ x 8½, 176 pp, Quality PB, 978-1-59473-231-7 **$16.99**

Writing—The Sacred Art: Beyond the Page to Spiritual Practice
By Rami Shapiro and Aaron Shapiro 5½ x 8½, 192 pp, Quality PB, 978-1-59473-372-7 **$16.99**

Women's Interest

There's a Woman in the Pulpit: Christian Clergywomen Share Their Hard Days, Holy Moments & the Healing Power of Humor
Edited by Rev. Martha Spong; Foreword by Rev. Carol Howard Merritt
Offers insight into the lives of Christian clergywomen and the rigors that come with commitment to religious life, representing fourteen denominations as well as dozens of seminaries and colleges. 6 x 9, 240 pp, Quality PB, 978-1-59473-588-2 **$18.99**

She Lives! Sophia Wisdom Works in the World
By Rev. Jann Aldredge-Clanton, PhD
Fascinating narratives of clergy and laypeople who are changing the institutional church and society by restoring biblical female divine names and images to Christian theology, worship symbolism and liturgical language.
6 x 9, 320 pp, Quality PB, 978-1-59473-573-8 **$18.99**

Birthing God: Women's Experiences of the Divine
By Lana Dalberg; Foreword by Kathe Schaaf
Powerful narratives of suffering, love and hope that inspire both personal and collective transformation. 6 x 9, 304 pp, Quality PB, 978-1-59473-480-9 **$18.99**

Women, Spirituality and Transformative Leadership
Where Grace Meets Power
Edited by Kathe Schaaf, Kay Lindahl, Kathleen S. Hurty, PhD, and Reverend Guo Cheen
A dynamic conversation on the power of women's spiritual leadership and its emerging patterns of transformation.
6 x 9, 288 pp, Quality PB, 978-1-59473-548-6 **$18.99**; HC, 978-1-59473-313-0 **$24.99**

Spiritually Healthy Divorce: Navigating Disruption with Insight & Hope
By Carolyne Call A spiritual map to help you move through the twists and turns of divorce. 6 x 9, 224 pp, Quality PB, 978-1-59473-288-1 **$16.99**

Bread, Body, Spirit: Finding the Sacred in Food
Edited and with Introductions by Alice Peck 6 x 9, 224 pp, Quality PB, 978-1-59473-242-3 **$19.99**

Dance—The Sacred Art: The Joy of Movement as a Spiritual Practice
By Cynthia Winton-Henry 5½ x 8½, 224 pp, Quality PB, 978-1-59473-268-3 **$16.99**

Daughters of the Desert: Stories of Remarkable Women from Christian, Jewish and Muslim Traditions *By Claire Rudolf Murphy, Meghan Nuttall Sayres, Mary Cronk Farrell, Sarah Conover and Betsy Wharton*
5½ x 8½, 192 pp, Illus., Quality PB, 978-1-59473-106-8 **$18.99** Inc. reader's discussion guide

The Divine Feminine in Biblical Wisdom Literature
Selections Annotated & Explained
Translation & Annotation by Rabbi Rami Shapiro; Foreword by Rev. Cynthia Bourgeault, PhD
5½ x 8½, 240 pp, Quality PB, 978-1-59473-109-9 **$18.99**

Divining the Body: Reclaim the Holiness of Your Physical Self
By Jan Phillips 8 x 8, 256 pp, Quality PB, 978-1-59473-080-1 **$18.99**

Honoring Motherhood: Prayers, Ceremonies & Blessings
Edited and with Introductions by Lynn L. Caruso
5 x 7¼, 272 pp, Quality PB, 978-1-58473-384-0 **$9.99**; HC, 978-1-59473-239-3 **$19.99**

New Feminist Christianity: Many Voices, Many Views
Edited by Mary E. Hunt and Diann L. Neu
6 x 9, 384 pp, Quality PB, 978-1-59473-435-9 **$19.99**; HC, 978-1-59473-285-0 **$24.99**

Next to Godliness: Finding the Sacred in Housekeeping
Edited by Alice Peck 6 x 9, 224 pp, Quality PB, 978-1-59473-214-0 **$19.99**

The Triumph of Eve & Other Subversive Bible Tales
By Matt Biers-Ariel 5½ x 8½, 192 pp, Quality PB, 978-1-59473-176-1 **$14.99**

Woman Spirit Awakening in Nature: Growing Into the Fullness of Who You Are
By Nancy Barrett Chickerneo, PhD; Foreword by Eileen Fisher
8 x 8, 224 pp, b/w illus., Quality PB, 978-1-59473-250-8 **$16.99**

Women of Color Pray: Voices of Strength, Faith, Healing, Hope and Courage
Edited and with Introductions by Christal M. Jackson 5 x 7¼, 208 pp, Quality PB, 978-1-59473-077-1 **$15.99**

Prayer / Meditation

The Advent of God's Word
Listening for the Power of the Divine Whisper—A Daily Retreat &
Devotional *By Rev. Dr. Brenda K. Buckwell, Obl. OSB*
For those who find themselves struggling with no time for prayer during the busy
Advent season. Step-by-step creative exercises help you celebrate the birth of Jesus.
6 x 9, 208 pp, Quality PB, 978-1-59473-576-9 **$16.99**

Calling on God
Inclusive Christian Prayers for Three Years of Sundays
By Peter Bankson and Deborah Sokolove
Prayers for today's world, vividly written for Christians who long for a way to
talk to and about God that feels fresh yet still connected to tradition.
6 x 9, 400 pp, Quality PB, 978-1-59473-568-4 **$18.99**
The Worship Leader's Guide to Calling on God
8½ x 11, 20 pp, PB, 978-1-59473-591-2 **$9.99**

Openings, 2nd Edition
A Daybook of Saints, Sages, Psalms and Prayer Practices
By Rev. Larry J. Peacock
For anyone hungry for a richer prayer life, this prayer book offers daily inspiration to help you move closer to God. Draws on a wide variety of resources—lives
of saints and sages from every age, psalms, and suggestions for personal reflection
and practice. 6 x 9, 448 pp, Quality PB, 978-1-59473-545-5 **$18.99**

Openings: A Daybook of Saints, Sages, Psalms and
Prayer Practices—Leader's Guide 8½ x 11, 12 pp, PB, 978-1-59473-572-1 **$9.99**
Honest to God Prayer: Spirituality as Awareness, Empowerment,
Relinquishment and Paradox *By Kent Ira Groff*
6 x 9, 192 pp, Quality PB, 978-1-59473-433-5 **$16.99**

Lectio Divina—**The Sacred Art**
Transforming Words & Images into Heart-Centered Prayer
By Christine Valters Paintner, PhD 5½ x 8½, 240 pp, Quality PB, 978-1-59473-300-0 **$16.99**
Men Pray: Voices of Strength, Faith, Healing, Hope and Courage
Created by the Editors at SkyLight Paths; With Introductions by Brian D. McLaren
5 x 7¼, 192 pp, HC, 978-1-59473-395-6 **$16.99**
Secrets of Prayer: A Multifaith Guide to Creating Personal Prayer in Your Life
By Nancy Corcoran, CSJ 6 x 9, 160 pp, Quality PB, 978-1-59473-215-7 **$16.99**
Women of Color Pray: Voices of Strength, Faith, Healing, Hope and Courage
Edited and with Introductions by Christal M. Jackson
5 x 7¼, 208 pp, Quality PB, 978-1-59473-077-1 **$15.99**

Prayer / M. Basil Pennington, ocso

Finding Grace at the Center, 3rd Edition: The Beginning of
Centering Prayer *With Thomas Keating, OCSO, and Thomas E. Clarke, SJ*
Foreword by Rev. Cynthia Bourgeault, PhD A practical guide to a simple and beautiful
form of meditative prayer. 5 x 7¼, 128 pp, Quality PB, 978-1-59473-182-2 **$12.99**

The Monks of Mount Athos: A Western Monk's Extraordinary
Spiritual Journey on Eastern Holy Ground *Foreword by Archimandrite Dionysios*
Explores the landscape, monastic communities and food of Athos.
6 x 9, 352 pp, Quality PB, 978-1-893361-78-2 **$18.95**

Psalms: A Spiritual Commentary *Illus. by Phillip Ratner*
Reflections on some of the most beloved passages from the Bible's most widely
read book. 6 x 9, 176 pp, 24 full-page b/w illus., Quality PB, 978-1-59473-234-8 **$16.99**

The Song of Songs: A Spiritual Commentary *Illus. by Phillip Ratner*
Explore the Bible's most challenging mystical text.
6 x 9, 160 pp, 14 full-page b/w illus., Quality PB, 978-1-59473-235-5 **$16.99**
HC, 978-1-59473-004-7 **$19.99**

Spirituality / Animal Companions

Blessing the Animals
Prayers and Ceremonies to Celebrate God's Creatures, Wild and Tame
Edited and with Introductions by Lynn L. Caruso
5 x 7¼, 256 pp, Quality PB, 978-1-59473-253-9 **$15.99**; HC, 978-1-59473-145-7 **$19.99**

Remembering My Pet
A Kid's Own Spiritual Workbook for When a Pet Dies
By Nechama Liss-Levinson, PhD, and Rev. Molly Phinney Baskette, MDiv
Foreword by Lynn L. Caruso
8 x 10, 48 pp, 2-color text, HC, 978-1-59473-221-8 **$16.99**

What Animals Can Teach Us about Spirituality
Inspiring Lessons from Wild and Tame Creatures
By Diana L. Guerrero 6 x 9, 176 pp, Quality PB, 978-1-893361-84-3 **$18.99**

Spirituality & Crafts

The Advent of God's Word
Listening for the Power of the Divine Whisper—A Daily Retreat &
Devotional *By Rev. Dr. Brenda K. Buckwell, Obl. OSB*
For those who find themselves struggling with no time for prayer during the
busy Advent season. Step-by-step creative exercises help you celebrate the birth
of Jesus and enter the new calendar year with a personal pictorial journal of
the season. 6 x 9, 208 pp, Quality PB, 978-1-59473-576-9 **$16.99**

Beading—The Creative Spirit
Finding Your Sacred Center through the Art of Beadwork
By Rev. Wendy Ellsworth
Invites you on a spiritual pilgrimage into the kaleidoscope world of
glass and color. 7 x 9, 240 pp, 8-page color insert, 40+ b/w photos and 40 diagrams
Quality PB, 978-1-59473-267-6 **$18.99**

Contemplative Crochet
A Hands-On Guide for Interlocking Faith and Craft
By Cindy Crandall-Frazier; Foreword by Linda Skolnik
Illuminates the spiritual lessons you can learn through crocheting.
7 x 9, 208 pp, b/w photos, Quality PB, 978-1-59473-238-6 **$16.99**

The Knitting Way
A Guide to Spiritual Self-Discovery
By Linda Skolnik and Janice MacDaniels
Examines how you can explore and strengthen your spiritual life through knitting.
7 x 9, 240 pp, b/w photos, Quality PB, 978-1-59473-079-5 **$16.99**

The Painting Path
Embodying Spiritual Discovery through Yoga, Brush and Color
By Linda Novick; Foreword by Richard Segalman
Explores the divine connection you can experience through art.
7 x 9, 208 pp, 8-page color insert, plus b/w photos, Quality PB, 978-1-59473-226-3 **$18.99**

The Soulwork of Clay
A Hands-On Approach to Spirituality
By Marjory Zoet Bankson; Photos by Peter Bankson
Takes you through the seven-step process of making clay into a pot, drawing
parallels at each stage to the process of spiritual growth.
7 x 9, 192 pp, b/w photos, Quality PB, 978-1-59473-249-2 **$16.99**

The Quilting Path: A Guide to Spiritual Discovery through Fabric, Thread and Kabbalah
By Louise Silk 7 x 9, 192 pp, b/w photos and illus., Quality PB, 978-1-59473-206-5 **$16.99**

The Scrapbooking Journey: A Hands-On Guide to Spiritual Discovery
By Cory Richardson-Lauve; Foreword by Stacy Julian
7 x 9, 176 pp, 8-page color insert, plus b/w photos, Quality PB, 978-1-59473-216-4 **$18.99**

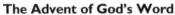

Spirituality

Mere Spirituality
The Spiritual Life According to Henri Nouwen
By Wil Hernandez, PhD, Obl. OSB; Foreword by Ronald Rolheiser
Introduction to Nouwen's spiritual thought, distills key insights on the realm of the spiritual life into one concise and compelling overview of his spirituality of the heart.
6 x 9, 160 pp, Quality PB, 978-1-59473-586-8 **$16.99**

The Forgiveness Handbook
Spiritual Wisdom and Practice for the Journey to Freedom, Healing and Peace
Created by the Editors at SkyLight Paths; Introduction by The Rev. Canon Marianne Wells Borg
Offers inspiration, encouragement and spiritual practice from across faith traditions for all who seek hope, wholeness and the freedom that comes from true forgiveness.
6 x 9, 256 pp, Quality PB, 978-1-59473-577-6 **$18.99**

Like a Child
Restoring the Awe, Wonder, Joy and Resiliency of the Human Spirit
By Rev. Timothy J. Mooney
By breaking free from our misperceptions about what it means to be an adult, we can reshape our world and become harbingers of grace. This unique spiritual resource explores Jesus's counsel to become like children in order to enter the kingdom of God. 6 x 9, 160 pp, Quality PB, 978-1-59473-543-1 **$16.99**

The Passionate Jesus: What We Can Learn from Jesus about Love, Fear, Grief, Joy and Living Authentically
By The Rev. Peter Wallace
Reveals Jesus as a passionate figure who was involved, present, connected, honest and direct with others and encourages you to build personal authenticity in every area of your own life. 6 x 9, 208 pp, Quality PB, 978-1-59473-393-2 **$18.99**

Gathering at God's Table: The Meaning of Mission in the Feast of Faith
By Katharine Jefferts Schori
A profound reminder of our role in the larger frame of God's dream for a restored and reconciled world. 6 x 9, 256 pp, HC, 978-1-59473-316-1 **$21.99**

The Heartbeat of God: Finding the Sacred in the Middle of Everything
By Katharine Jefferts Schori; Foreword by Joan Chittister, OSB
Explores our connections to other people, to other nations and with the environment through the lens of faith.
6 x 9, 240 pp, HC, 978-1-59473-292-8 **$21.99**; Quality PB, 978-1-59473-589-9 **$16.99**

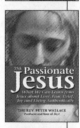

Laugh Your Way to Grace: Reclaiming the Spiritual Power of Humor
By Rev. Susan Sparks
A powerful, humorous case for laughter as a spiritual, healing path.
6 x 9, 176 pp, Quality PB, 978-1-59473-280-5 **$16.99**

Claiming Earth as Common Ground: The Ecological Crisis through the Lens of Faith
By Andrea Cohen-Kiener; Foreword by Rev. Sally Bingham
6 x 9, 192 pp, Quality PB, 978-1-59473-261-4 **$16.99**

Living into Hope: A Call to Spiritual Action for Such a Time as This
By Rev. Dr. Joan Brown Campbell; Foreword by Karen Armstrong
6 x 9, 208 pp, Quality PB, 978-1-59473-436-6 **$18.99**; HC, 978-1-59473-283-6 **$21.99**

Renewal in the Wilderness
A Spiritual Guide to Connecting with God in the Natural World
By John Lionberger 6 x 9, 176 pp, b/w photos, Quality PB, 978-1-59473-219-5 **$16.99**

A Walk with Four Spiritual Guides: Krishna, Buddha, Jesus, and Ramakrishna
By Andrew Harvey 5½ x 8½, 192 pp, b/w photos & illus., Quality PB, 978-1-59473-138-9 **$18.99**

About SKYLIGHT PATHS Publishing

SkyLight Paths Publishing is creating a place where people of different spiritual traditions come together for challenge and inspiration, a place where we can help each other understand the mystery that lies at the heart of our existence.

Through spirituality, our religious beliefs are increasingly becoming a part of our lives—rather than *apart* from our lives. While many of us may be more interested than ever in spiritual growth, we may be less firmly planted in traditional religion. Yet, we do want to deepen our relationship to the sacred, to learn from our own as well as from other faith traditions, and to practice in new ways.

SkyLight Paths sees both believers and seekers as a community that increasingly transcends traditional boundaries of religion and denomination—people wanting to learn from each other, *walking together, finding the way.*

For your information and convenience, at the back of this book we have provided a list of other SkyLight Paths books you might find interesting and useful. They cover the following subjects:

Buddhism / Zen	Gnosticism	Poetry
Catholicism	Hinduism / Vedanta	Prayer
Chaplaincy	Inspiration	Religious Etiquette
Children's Books	Islam / Sufism	Retirement & Later-Life Spirituality
Christianity	Judaism	Spiritual Biography
Comparative Religion	Meditation	Spiritual Direction
Earth-Based Spirituality	Mindfulness	Spirituality
Enneagram	Monasticism	Women's Interest
Global Spiritual Perspectives	Mysticism	Worship
	Personal Growth	

Or phone, fax, mail or email to: SKYLIGHT PATHS Publishing
Sunset Farm Offices, Route 4 • P.O. Box 237 • Woodstock, Vermont 05091
Tel: (802) 457-4000 • Fax: (802) 457-4004 • www.skylightpaths.com
Credit card orders: (800) 962-4544 (8:30AM–5:30PM EST Monday–Friday)
Generous discounts on quantity orders. SATISFACTION GUARANTEED. Prices subject to change.

For more information about each book,
visit our website at www.skylightpaths.com.